Student **2A** Book

Apple Pie

Delta's Beginning ESL Program

Sadae Iwataki, Editor

Jean Owensby

Constance Turner

Greta Kojima

Joanne Abing

Jayme Adelson-Goldstein

REVISED EDITION

© 1994 by Delta Systems Co., Inc.
Revised Edition 1995

ISBN 0–937354–58–9

Production Staff:	Geoff Hill
	Diane Bergeron
	Linda Bruell
	Jeannie Patchin
Cover Design:	Geoff Hill
Illustrations:	Jim Ruskowski
	Donna Lewis
	Laura Heuer

Delta Systems Co., Inc.
1400 Miller Parkway
McHenry, IL 60050 U.S.A.

Apple Pie 2A
Table of Contents

Communication Objectives:
>   Identify various breakfast foods
>   Ask about and discuss preferences
>   Use a food pyramid to assess a healthy diet

Structures:
>   Imperatives
>   Simple present
>   Negative *anything*

Communication Objectives:
>   Talk about meals and snacks
>   Extend an invitation
>   Accept/refuse an invitation

New Structures:
>   *Would like* + noun
>   *Would like* + verb
>   Contrast of *Do you like* and *Would you like*

Communication Objectives:
>   Order/serve food
>   Tell server how you want food prepared
>   Discuss tasks to prepare for a party

New Structures:
>   Questions with *how*

Unit One

The Foods We Eat

Lesson 1

A Healthy Diet

Objectives: In this lesson you will learn to discuss and follow a healthy diet.

Opening: Greeting Old and New Friends

Walk around the room.

Greet two old friends.

Meet two new friends.

Examples: **Old Friends**

S1: Hi, *Sara*. It's good to see you!

S2: Hi, *Tony*. How are you?

S1: I'm fine.

[Note: When we see friends after an absence, we can say "Good to see you!" or "Nice to see you again!"]

New Friends

S1: Hi! My name's *May Lei*.

S2: My name's *Emiko Sato*.

S1: I'm happy to meet you, *Emiko*.

S2: And I'm glad to meet you, *May*.

Something New: What's for Breakfast?
Listen and Look

Here are four typical breakfasts. Which breakfast do you like?

coffee and doughnuts

cereal, banana, bran muffin, and milk

orange juice, eggs, bacon,
hash–browned potatoes, toast, coffee

grapefruit, pancakes, ham, coffee

☛ Practice: "What's your favorite breakfast?"

1. S1: What's your favorite breakfast?
   S2: (My favorite breakfast is)
   Bacon and eggs.

2. S1: What do you eat for breakfast?
   S2: I don't eat anything.
   I just drink coffee.

3. S1: Do you eat breakfast every day?
   S2: No, I don't. I don't have time.

4. S1: What does Jim eat for breakfast?
   S2: He eats cereal.

Let's Talk: Eat Some Breakfast

It's a weekday morning. Luisa is rushing to school.

Luisa: Bye, Mom. I'm going now.

Mrs. Garcia: Eat some breakfast first, Luisa.

Luisa: I can't. I'm late for school.

Mrs. Garcia: Take this banana and muffin with you.

Discussion

1. Is breakfast an important meal?
2. What kind of breakfast do parents want for their children?
3. Do children always eat a good breakfast?
4. Do you eat breakfast every day?
5. What do you eat for breakfast?

☞ Practice: "I can't. I'm late"

1. S1: Eat some cereal, Jim.
   S2: I can't. I'm late.

2. S1: Take this muffin with you.
   S2: All right.

☞ Practice Activity: What do you have for breakfast?

1. Ask four students about their breakfasts.

   Example: "What do you have for breakfast every day?"
   "I have milk and toast."

2. Write the answers on the chart.

NAME	Breakfast	
	Eat	Drink
	doughnut	*coffee*

Something New: Foods for a Healthy Diet

The Food Pyramid

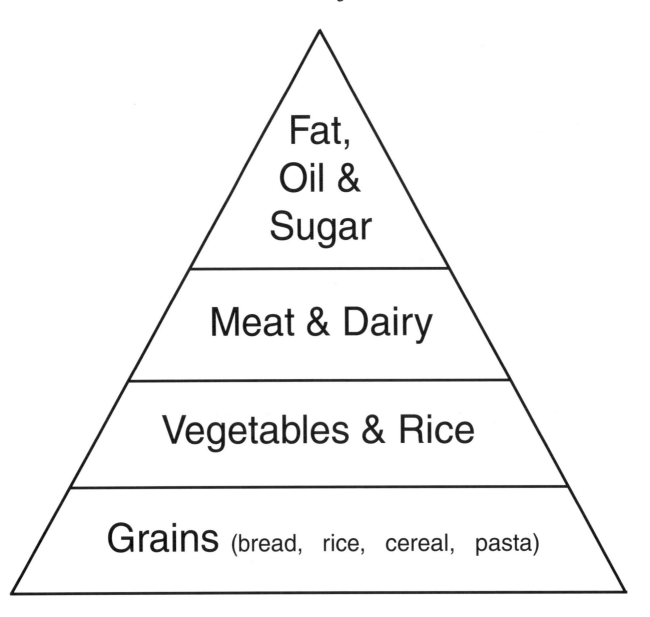

Discussion

1. A pyramid has a strong base. What food group is at the "base" of the pyramid?
2. What are the next most important foods? The third?
3. Why are fat, oil, and sugar at the top of the pyramid?
4. What are some foods in each group?
5. What does it mean to eat a "balanced" diet?

☛ Practice Activity

1. Look at the pictures and name the foods.
2. List the words on the board and on the lines below.
3. Add foods in each group from your country.
4. Tell the class about the foods from your country.

1. Grains: Bread, Rice, Cereal, Pasta

_____

_____

_____

2. Vegetables, Fruits

_____

_____

_____

3. Meat and Dairy Foods

_____

_____

_____

4. Fat, Oil, Sugar

_____

_____

_____

☛ **Practice: "Is that a healthy breakfast?"**

1. S1: What do you eat for breakfast?
   S2: A hamburger.
   S1: Is that a healthy breakfast?
   S2: I think so.

2. S1: What's a healthy breakfast for you?
   S2: Cereal, milk, toast, and fruit juice.
   S1: Do you eat a healthy breakfast every day?
   S2: I try.

Reading: A Good Diet

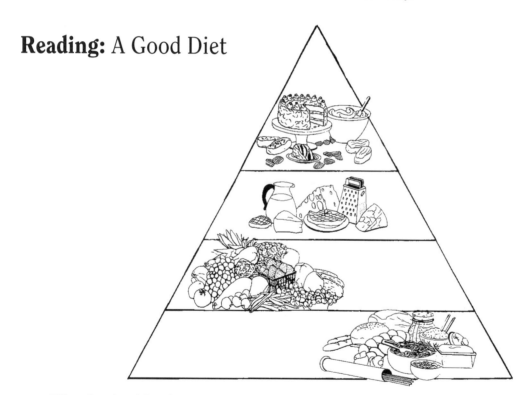

What is a healthy diet? A good diet includes grains, fruits, vegetables, and sometimes milk and meat foods.

Americans eat many different kinds of food each day. They eat Italian, Mexican, Chinese, Japanese, Thai, and French food. And American food, of course.

Today more people are trying to eat a healthy diet. They try to include food from all the food groups every day.

Discussion

1. What is a healthy diet?
2. What kinds of food do many Americans eat?
3. What are people trying to do about food?
4. What kinds of food do you eat?
5. Do you think you have a good diet?
6. Food with a lot of fat, oil, or sugar in it is called "junk food." Do you eat a lot of junk food? (Junk food isn't very good for you, but it tastes good!)

✐ Writing

1. What do you usually eat for breakfast?

   _____

2. What's a typical breakfast in your country?

   _____

3. What are your favorite foods from your country?

   _____

4. Do you eat a healthy diet? If not, what do you need to change?

   _____

   _____

5. Do you think Americans follow a healthy diet? Why or why not?

   _____

   _____

   _____

✍✍ More Writing

1. Make a list of everything you ate yesterday.

    _____   _____

    _____   _____

    _____   _____

    _____   _____

    _____   _____

    _____   _____

2. Now write the foods in the chart below. Put each food in the correct food group.
3. Discuss your chart with a partner. How many foods are there in each group? Is that good or bad?

Yesterday's Food			
Grains	**Vegetables, Fruits**	**Milk, Meat**	**Fat, Oil, Sugar**

Lesson 1 Activity Page

A. Listen and check the food groups you hear.

	Milk and Meat	Fruits / Vegetables	Bread
1.	✓	✓	✓
2.			
3.			
4.			
5.			
6.			

Now look at the chart. How many of the meals are balanced?

B. Read the meals below.

1. Decide whether the meals are healthy or unhealthy, and why.
2. Discuss your answers with your partner.

		Healthy	Unhealthy	Why?
1.	Coffee and doughnut		✗	*too much oil*
2.	Hot dog, popcorn, and cola			
3.	Hamburger and french fries			
4.	Small salad with chicken and cheese			
5.	Apple, cheese, and crackers			
6.	Banana and peanut butter sandwich			
7.	Chicken, potato, and carrots			
8.	Steak, rice, and ice cream			

Light Meals, Heavy Meals

Objectives: In this lesson you will learn to talk about meals and eating habits.

✓ Review: A Good Diet

1. Name and list on the board some of the foods in the food pyramid. Explain what the pyramid means.
2. Discuss the foods. What foods do you like? Dislike?

Something New: Three Meals a Day

a light breakfast

a heavy breakfast

a light lunch

a heavy lunch

a light dinner

a heavy dinner

☛ Practice: "Are you a big eater?"

1. S1: Are you a big eater?
   S2: No, I'm not. I eat a big breakfast, but I eat a light lunch and dinner.

2. S1: Is your husband a big eater?
   S2: Yes, he is. He eats three heavy meals a day.

Let's Talk: Are You on a Diet?

Norman: Would you like to go out for a hamburger?

Sara: Thanks, but I have a sack lunch today. Yogurt and an apple.

Norman: Are you on a diet?

Sara: Yes. I'm trying to lose a few pounds, but it's difficult. I eat a heavy dinner with the family every night.

☛ **Practice: "What's for lunch?"**

1. S1: Are you on a diet?

    S2: Yes, I am.

    S1: What do you have for lunch today?

    S2: (I have) Cottage cheese and a tomato.

2. S1: Is Lou on a diet?

    S2: Yes, he is.

    S1: What's he having for dinner today?

    S2: (He's having) A chicken salad.

3. S1: Would you like to go out for lunch?

    S2: I'd love to. Let's get a pizza.

4. S1: Would you like to go out for lunch?

    S2: Sorry, but I'm not having lunch. I'm on a diet.

    S1: Okay.

Something New: Snacks

popcorn   potato chips   a candy bar

cookies   a piece of pie   nuts

an apple   a soft drink   an ice cream cone

1. Do you like to eat between meals?
2. When do you eat snacks?
3. What are your favorite snacks?

★ Something Extra: What Do You Like/What Would You Like Now?

Ben: What do you like to eat for lunch?

May: I like to eat salads.

Ben: Would you like a salad today?

May: No, I'm hungry today. I'd like a
      hamburger and french fries.

☛ **Practice: "I'd like some water"**

1. S1: What do you like to drink with your meals?

    S2: Coffee.

    S1: Would you like a cup of coffee now?

    S2: No, I'd like some water today.

2. S1: What do you like to have for snacks?

    S2: Candy or cookies.

    S1: Would you like a candy bar?

    S2: Oh, I'd love it. Thanks.

Reading: American Coffee Shops

American coffee shops serve more than just coffee. They serve breakfast, lunch, and dinner.

You can have a light breakfast of just coffee and a sweet roll, or you can order a heavy breakfast of bacon, eggs, and pancakes. Sandwiches and salads are popular for lunch.

Coffee shops serve chicken, fish, or meat for dinner. Coffee shops are restaurants, but they serve inexpensive meals. Some coffee shops are open 24 hours a day, seven days a week. They never close.

Discussion

1. What can you eat in an American coffee shop?
2. What do people like to eat for lunch?
3. Do you have coffee shops in your country? What kinds of food do they serve?
4. Do you like to eat in coffee shops? At fast–food restaurants?

✍ Writing

Answer the questions:

1. Do you like to eat in coffee shops? _____

2. Do you prefer to eat in a coffee shop or a fast–food restaurant? _____

   _____

3. Ask another student Question #2. Write his/her preference. _____

   _____

4. List your favorite foods:

Breakfast	Lunch	Dinner
_____	_____	_____
_____	_____	_____
_____	_____	_____
_____	_____	_____
_____	_____	_____
_____	_____	_____
_____	_____	_____
_____	_____	_____
_____	_____	_____

Lesson 2 Activity Pages

A. Listen to the meals and check light or heavy.

Light   Heavy

1. ✔ _____   _____

2. _____   _____

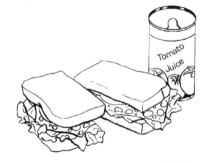

3. _____   _____

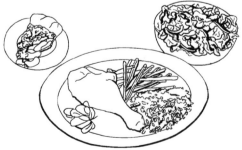

4. _____   _____

5. _____   _____

B. Write a new menu.

Sara is on a diet. Look at her family's dinner menu. Cross out the foods you think are bad for her. Write a new menu for Sara to help her lose a few pounds.

Sara's Original Menu	Sara's New Menu
Fried chicken	_____
French fries	_____
Coleslaw	_____
Ice cream	_____
Cola	_____

C. Write the missing words.

apple	big	diet	dinner	had	heavy	light	lunch	meals	pounds

Sara is on a _____*diet*_____.

She doesn't eat heavy _____

for breakfast or _____ because

she wants to lose five _____.

Today Sara's having a _____

lunch. For breakfast she _____ an

_____ and some yogurt. It's

difficult for Sara to diet at _____

time because her family likes to eat a

_____ dinner.

D. Work in a group. Ask and answer the questions.

What's your favorite... ?							
Name	**meat**	**vegetable**	**fruit**	**drink**	**salad**	**dessert**	**snack**

E. Work in a group. Look at your group's answers for exercise D, and plan a dinner menu for your group.

Balance your menu with foods from the different food groups.

Salad   _____

Main Course   _____

Vegetable(s)   _____

Dessert   _____

Beverage   _____

Notes

Eating Out

Objectives: In this lesson you will learn to order or serve food in a restaurant.

✔ **Review:** Eating Habits

Your Daily Diet

What do you like to eat for breakfast?
                    for lunch?
                    for dinner?

Snacks

Name some snacks and list on the board.
What are some favorite snacks of students?

Something New: Ordering Food

Eggs

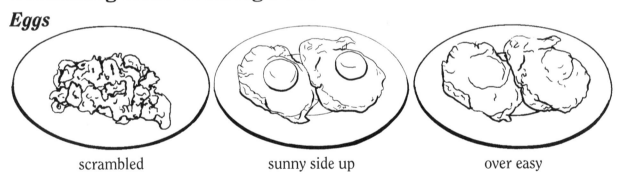

scrambled   sunny side up   over easy

Steak

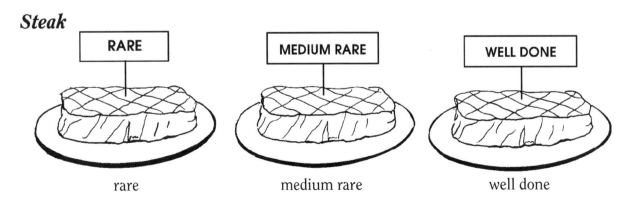

rare   medium rare   well done

Coffee

black   with sugar   with cream and sugar

Tea

plain   with lemon   with milk and sugar

Let's Talk: How Would You Like Your Steak?

Sara and Tomas are celebrating their anniversary with dinner at a restaurant.

Waiter: Good evening. Our specials tonight are sea bass and roast chicken.

Sara: I'd like the sea bass.

Tomas: I'd like a New York steak.

Waiter: How would you like your steak?

Tomas: Medium rare, please.

☛ Practice: "I'd like it well done"

1. S1: How would you like your steak?
   S2: Well done, please.

2. S1: How does Tom like his eggs?
   S2: Sunny side up.

3. S1: Would you like cream and sugar
       for your coffee?
   S2: Yes, thank you.

4. S1: How do you like your coffee?
   S2: Black, please.

Reading: A Potluck Party

Mario and Carol are in their new apartment now. They would like to have a party for their new apartment, but their new baby is keeping them very busy. So they are planning a potluck party. The guests bring some food to a potluck party, and the hosts provide some food, too.

Discussion

1. Why are Mario and Carol planning a potluck party?
2. Do you go to potluck parties?
3. What do you like to take to a potluck party?

☛ Practice Activity: Do you like eggs?

With a partner, ask and answer questions about your food likes.

> *Example:* Do you like eggs? How do you like your eggs?
>
> Do you drink tea? How do you like your tea?

✍ Writing

Write a short paragraph about eating out. Tell when you eat out, where you like to eat, what you like to eat, and how you like your food and drink.

_____

_____

_____

_____

_____

_____

_____

A. Listen to the order. Circle the correct information on the menu pad.

1.

JOE'S

Sandwiches

Hamburger
rare
medium
well done

Steak
rare
medium
well done

Chicken

Side Orders
Cole Slaw
Green Salad
French Fries
sm med lg

Drinks
Cola
sm med lg
Lemon–lime
sm med lg
Orange
sm med lg
Coffee
cream sugar
sm med lg
Tea
lemon sugar
sm med lg

2.

JOE'S

Sandwiches

Hamburger
rare
medium
well done

Steak
rare
medium
well done

Chicken

Side Orders
Cole Slaw
Green Salad
French Fries
sm med lg

Drinks
Cola
sm med lg
Lemon–lime
sm med lg
Orange
sm med lg
Coffee
cream sugar
sm med lg
Tea
lemon sugar
sm med lg

3.

JOE'S

Sandwiches

Hamburger
rare
medium
well done

Steak
rare
medium
well done

Chicken

Side Orders
Cole Slaw
Green Salad
French Fries
sm med lg

Drinks
Cola
sm med lg
Lemon–lime
sm med lg
Orange
sm med lg
Coffee
cream sugar
sm med lg
Tea
lemon sugar
sm med lg

B. Walk around the classroom and find someone who...

Name

1. likes to eat scrambled eggs: _____

2. likes to drink coffee with sugar: _____

3. likes to eat well–done steak: _____

4. likes to eat fresh fish: _____

5. likes to drink tea with lemon: _____

6. likes to drink black coffee: _____

C. Make three sentences from the information you have.

Example:

Juana likes to eat scrambled eggs. _____

1. _____

2. _____

3. _____

Notes

Name _____ Date _____

Unit One  Evaluation

I. Listening Comprehension

Listen and circle the correct answer, A or B.

1.

A   B   2.   A   B

3.

A   B   4.   A   B

5.

A. Yes, I am.   B. Yes, I do.   6.   A. No, it isn't.   B. No, it doesn't.

7.

A   B

II. Reading

Circle the correct answers.

1. I'm on a diet. I eat a _____
   lunch every day.

       light   heavy   big

2. She likes her steak _____.

       well done   over easy   black

3. _____ is in the grain group.

       rice   fish   bananas

4. What would you like to have for a
   snack today? I _____ an apple.

       like   'd like   like to eat

III. Writing

Write the questions or answers.

1. How do you like your coffee?

   _____

2. _____

   _____?

   Scrambled.

3. _____
   to eat for lunch?
   I'd like to eat a hamburger.

4. Does he eat a heavy dinner?

   No, _____. He's on a diet.

Unit Two

Keep in Touch

Postal Services

Objectives: In this lesson you will learn to discuss and use post office services.

✔ Review: Eating Out

1. At a coffee shop: Take the roles of a waiter/waitress and customers ordering and serving breakfast.
2. At a restaurant: Take the roles of a waiter/waitress and customers ordering a special occasion dinner at a restaurant.

Something New: Postal Services

Letter Mail

First Class mail for the U.S. costs 32 cents.

A postcard for the U.S. costs 20 cents.

A First Class stamp for Mexico costs 35 cents.

International Airmail costs 50 cents.

An aerogram for international mail costs 45 cents.

Discussion

1. What is First Class mail? Is it the same as airmail?
2. When do you write postcards instead of letters?
3. What is an aerogram? Is it more or less expensive than a letter? Why?
4. How do you send mail to your country, by letter or by aerogram?

Let's Talk: First Class Mail Goes by Air

Tranh has letters for friends in Mexico City and relatives in Seattle.

Tranh: I'd like an Airmail stamp for Seattle, please.

Clerk: You need a First Class stamp. All First Class mail goes by air.

Tranh: I'd like 10 First Class stamps and I'd like five Airmail stamps for Mexico City, too.

Clerk: 10 thirty–two cent stamps and 5 thirty–five cent stamps. That's $4.95.

☛ Practice: "It's a 32–cent stamp"

1. S1: What's that?
      S2: It's a 32–cent stamp.

2. S1: How much is an international Airmail stamp?

      S2: It's fifty cents.

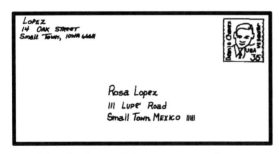

3. S1: Is that a 50–cent stamp?
      S2: No, it's a 35–cent stamp.

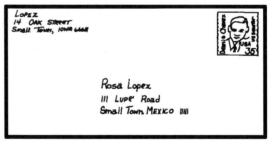

4. S1: Is a First Class stamp okay for Mexico?

      S2: No, you need a 35–cent stamp.

★ Something New: Packages

Parcel Post
(4–10 days)

Express Mail
(overnight)

Priority Mail
(2–3 days)

Discussion

1. Which is more expensive, Parcel Post or Priority Mail?
2. Is Express Mail expensive?
3. How long does Parcel Post to your country take? Priority Mail?

★ Something Extra: How to Send a Package

Jae Kim wants to send a vase to her mother in Korea.
Jim Garcia has a large photograph of his family to send to his grandparents in Mexico.
Each person is reading the post office directions for sending packages:

Post Office Directions	What Jae Does	What Jim Does
1. Choose the proper container.	She gets a strong box at the market.	He buys a large envelope.
2. Use newspaper, tissue, or other padding.	She gets old newspaper and cushions the vase.	He cuts cardboard to fit in the envelope.
3. Use strong tape or wrapping paper.	She puts strong tape around the box.	He puts tape on the envelope after he puts in the photo.
4. Address the package clearly.	She prints her mother's name and address and her return address on the box.	He prints his grandparent's name and address and his return address on the envelope.
5. At the post office, ask the clerk to stamp special instructions.	She asks the clerk to stamp "FRAGILE" on the box.	He asks the clerk to stamp "DO NOT BEND" on the envelope.

☛ Practice Activity: Send a Package

Discuss in small groups:

1. Does anyone in your group have an item to mail, either in the U.S. or overseas? What is it?
2. Give the person advice on how to prepare the package for mailing.

☛ Practice Activity: Which Service to Use?

The Need	The Service
1. A letter and a photograph for Seattle	___ Priority Mail
2. Short messages for 10 people	___ First Class
3. A package to go quickly	___ International Airmail
4. A package to go inexpensively	___ postcards
5. A letter and a photograph for Hong Kong	___ Parcel Post

Reading: A Money Order

Felix has a steady job. He works for a carpenter. He is learning to build cabinets and furniture.

Felix's parents live in El Salvador. They are old and cannot work. Felix tries to send a little money to them every month. A safe way to send money is a money order. Felix goes to the post office every month and buys a money order for his parents. He puts it in an envelope with a letter and sends it by International Airmail.

His parents are always happy to receive a letter from their son in the U.S.

Discussion

1. What kind of a job does Felix have?
2. What is he learning to do?
3. Where are Felix's parents?
4. How does Felix help his parents?
5. What is a safe way to send money by mail?
6. Do you send money to your country? How do you send it?

Reading: Felix's Letter

March 14, 1994

Dear Mom and Dad,

I am doing well in my job. I am learning to be a good carpenter. I can build cabinets and counters for kitchens. Last month I worked overtime and earned some extra money. I am sending you a money order.

On Sunday I visited Enrique and Susana Rivera. We talked and listened to music from El Salvador. It is good to have friends from home! In this letter there is a picture of me with Enrique and Susana.

Please write. I want to get a letter from home.

Your son,

Felix

✎ Writing: Write a Letter

1. Write a short letter to a friend or family member.
2. Follow correct letter writing form, with the date, salutation, and closing.
3. Suggestions: Write about what you are doing at work, what you did last weekend, what you want to do, etc.

_____

Dear _____

_____

_____

_____

_____

_____

_____

_____

_____

A. Listen and put the correct number under the person talking.

UNITED STATES
POST OFFICE

_____   _____   _1_   _____   _____

B. Look at the picture and write the correct words in the story below.

aerogram	Express Mail	letter	First Class	Five	package
Parcel Post	post office	aerograms	postcards	stamps	waiting

_____ people are standing in line at the _____ today.

They're all _____ for service. A young girl is waiting to mail _____.

The woman next to the young girl is sending an _____ to Venezuela. Her family lives in Venezuela so she always buys _____. The man in the suit is sending an important paper to New York. He needs to send his envelope by _____.

The young boy at the end of the line needs _____. He wants to send his letters _____. The woman at the front of the line is sending a _____ to her mother, for her mother's birthday. The package can go by _____ and get to her mother on time.

Unit Two | Lesson 5

I'm Homesick

Objectives: In this lesson you will learn to talk about how you feel and make suggestions to help.

✔ Review: Postal Services

1. Name some of the services offered by the post office.
2. Say the steps to prepare a package for mailing.
3. Discuss the best way to send money by mail.

Something New: What's the Matter?
Listen and Look

Problem

Suggestion

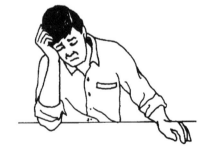

I'm sick.

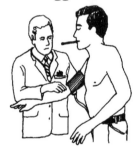

Go to the doctor.

I'm tired and sleepy.

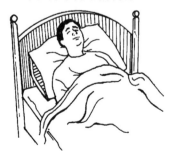

Go to bed early.

Problem	**Suggestion**

I'm thirsty.	Drink some water.

I'm hungry.	Eat something.

I'm cold.	Put on a sweater.

I'm warm.	Turn on the fan.

Let's Talk: I Want to Get a Letter from Home

May: Do you have a letter for me?

Mailman: No, I don't. I just have some junk mail for you.

May: Oh shucks! I really want to get a letter from home.

Mailman: You're homesick. Why don't you call home?

May: That's a good idea.

☛ Practice: "She wants to get a letter"

1. S1: Is Lola homesick?
   S2: Yes, she is. She wants to get a letter from home.
   S1: Why doesn't she call home?
   S2: That's a good idea.

2. S1: What's the matter?
   S2: I'm cold.
   S1: Put on this sweater.
   S2: Thank you.

3. S1: Is anything the matter?
   S2: I'm warm.
   S1: Why don't you turn on the fan?
   S2: That's a good idea.

4. S1: What's the matter?
   S2: I'm tired and sleepy.
   S1: Go to bed early tonight.
   S2: That's a good idea.

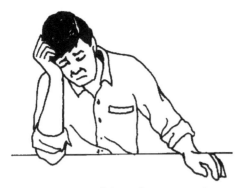
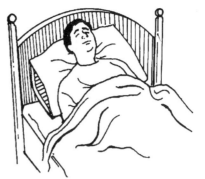

5. S1: Is something the matter?

   S2: Yes, I'm sick.

   S1: Why don't you go to the doctor?

   S2: That's a good idea.

6. S1: Is something the matter with John?

   S2: Yes, he's tired.

   S1: Why doesn't he go to bed?

   S2: That's a good idea.

■ Interaction: Making Suggestions

Walk around the room.

Tell each other your feelings or problems (if possible, make them real).

Make suggestions by saying "Why don't you - - - - - - - ?"

Reading: Send Mail

How do you mail your letters? Mr. and Mrs. Valdez are retired and don't go out much. They leave their letters in their mailbox. The mailman takes them to the post office.

Tony uses the mail collection boxes on street corners. He drops his letters in the bright blue mailboxes on his way to work. Mail trucks pick up the mail on the days and at the times listed on the schedule.

Tony's corner mailbox lists the schedule below:

Mail Collection Times					
Monday through Friday except holidays		Saturday		Sunday	
AM	PM	AM	PM	AM	PM
					12:30
8:15	1:50		1:00	Holidays	
11:30	4:30			AM	PM
				10:30	

Discussion

1. What do Mr. and Mrs. Valdez do with their letters?
2. Where does Tony mail his letters?
3. Where is the mail collection schedule on mailboxes?
4. Is there mail collection every day of the year at Tony's neighborhood mailbox?
5. How many times a day is the mail collection on Wednesdays? Fridays? Sundays?
6. Does every mailbox have daily collection?
7. How do you mail your letters?

☛ Practice Activity: Mail Collection Times

Check the mail collection schedule on page 43 and answer these questions.

1. Is there a mail pick–up on Saturday? What time?

   _____.

2. What time is the mail collection on holidays?

   _____.

3. It's 3:00 PM Wednesday. What time is the next collection?

   _____.

4. It's 4:50 Friday afternoon. When is the next collection?

   _____.

5. How many times a day is there mail collection on weekdays?

   _____.

✎ Writing

1. _____?

   I'm tired.

2. Is something the matter?

   _____.

3. Is something the matter?

   _____.

   _____

   _____?

   That's a good idea.

4. What's the matter?

   _____.

   _____

   put on this sweater?

   Thank you.

★ Something Extra: Junk Mail

Eliza is excited. She has a lot of mail. She is opening some of the mail now. Oh, no! It is all junk mail—nothing but ads and mail order catalogs.

Discussion

1. What is junk mail?
2. Why do you think we call it "junk mail?"
3. Do you receive junk mail?
4. Do you like to receive junk mail?
5. What do you do with your junk mail?
6. A task for tomorrow: Bring some samples of junk mail to share with the class.

Lesson 5 Activity Pages

A. Listen to the complaint and check the problem.

	Hungry	Thirsty	Tired	Hot	Cold	Sick
1. George	✓					
2. Walter						
3. Van						
4. Grace						
5. Jean						
6. Edith						

B. Talk with your partner.

Partner A look at this page. Partner B look at D on page 48. Ask and answer questions about the missing information.

What's the matter with...?	Problem	He/she needs to...
Harry	tired	go to bed early
Paula	_____	_____
Gladys	cold	_____
Max	_____	_____
Tina	hungry	_____

C. Match the problems and the suggestions.

1. I'm sick. _____   a. Turn on the fan.

2. I'm hungry. _____   b. Put on this sweater.

3. I'm thirsty. _____   c. Call home.

4. I'm homesick. _____   d. Go to the doctor.

5. I'm cold. _____   e. Go to bed early.

6. I'm hot. _____   f. Eat something.

7. I'm tired. _____   g. Drink some water.

D. Talk with your partner.

Partner B look at this page. Partner A look at B on page 47. Ask and answer questions about the missing information.

What's the matter with...?	Problem	He/she needs to...
Harry	tired	go to bed early
Paula	sick	_____
Gladys	_____	_____
Max	homesick	_____
Tina	_____	_____

E. Read the letters and write your answers.

Dear V. Helpful,

I'm getting married. I have a single apartment and my girlfriend lives with her parents. We don't have very much money. What can we do?

Thanh Phan

Dear V. Helpful,

I'm always late to work. I'm very tired and sleepy in the morning and it is difficult for me to wake up. My boss is getting angry. What can I do?

Miguel

1. Dear Phan,

Why don't you _____

_____

_____

_____

_____.

2. Dear Miguel,

Why don't you _____

_____

_____

_____

_____.

Dear V. Helpful,

I'm always hungry but I need to diet. My family likes big dinners and it's difficult to prepare their food and not eat it, too. What can I do?

Sara

3. Dear Sara,

Why don't you _____

_____

_____

_____

_____.

F. Talk about your suggestions to Thanh, Miguel, and Sara with the class.

I Need to Get Some Medicine

Objectives: In this lesson you will learn to give and follow directions and learn about items to buy in a drugstore.

✔ Review

How do You Feel?

Ask your partner how he or she feels and make suggestions to help.

> *Example:* S1: Is something the matter, (name)?
>
> S2: I'm tired today.
>
> S1: Why don't you take it easy?

Try to express real feelings. Other conditions are sick, sleepy, thirsty, hungry, cold, etc.

Junk Mail

Share with your group some samples of junk mail. Ask and answer questions.

> *Examples:* Is it attractive?
>
> Are you interested in the offer?
>
> Can you believe the ads?

Come together as a class and share the junk mail from your group.

Something New: A Drugstore

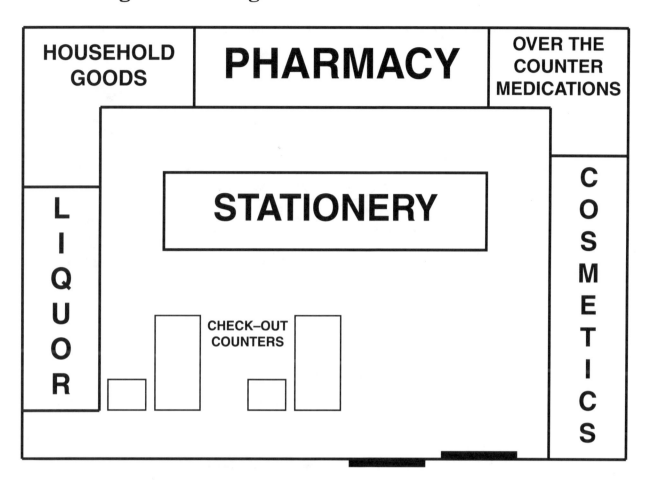

☛ **Practice Activity: Giving Directions**

I need to get...	Go to the...
some envelopes	stationery section
some lipstick	_____
some aspirin	_____
some laundry detergent	_____
some toothpaste	_____
some soft drinks	_____

Let's Talk: Go to the Pharmacy Section

Mrs. To has a prescription from her doctor. She is looking for the prescription department.

Mrs. To: Can you help me?
I need to get some medicine.

Clerk: Go to the pharmacy section.

Mrs. To: Where is it?

Clerk: It's in the back of the store.
Walk straight back from here.

Mrs. To: Thank you.

☛ Practice: "Go to the cosmetics section"

GREETING
CARDS

1. S1: What do you need to get?
   S2: I need to get some hand lotion.
   S1: Go to the cosmetics section.
       It's on the right.

2. S1: What do you need to get?
   S2: I need to get some greeting cards.
   S1: Go to the stationery section.
       It's in the center of the store.

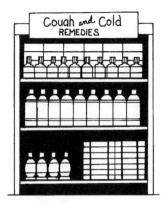

3. S1: What are you looking for?

    S2: I'm looking for some cough medicine.

    S1: Go to the back corner on your right.
    It's on aisle 10.

4. S1: Where are the soft drinks?

    S2: They're in the liquor department.

    S1: Where is it?

    S2: It's in the front of the store, on
    the left.

☛ Practice Activity: A Shopping List

1. Make a list of five items you need to buy at a drugstore.

2. Share your shopping list with your group.

3. Give each other directions on where to find all the items.

    Examples: comb, paper towels, beer, envelopes, toothpaste

Reading: American Drugstores

In many countries, people go to a pharmacy to buy their medicine. In the United States, people go to a drugstore. The American drugstore is like a supermarket. You can find many different things in these stores. You can buy cosmetics, housekeeping products, clothing, tools, liquor, toys, and even food products.

Oh, yes, they sell medicine, too. The pharmacy is usually in the corner, in the back of the store.

Discussion

1. Where do people buy medicine in many countries?

2. Where do people in the U.S. go for their medicine?

3. Why is an American drugstore like a supermarket?

4. Do some supermarkets sell drugstore items, too? What are they?

5. Can you buy medicine in a supermarket?

6. Where did you buy medicine in your country?

✍ Writing

Write questions or answers about the Reading.

1. Where do people in the U.S. go to buy medicine?

   _____.

2 _____?

   You can find many different things.

3. Can you buy food and clothing in a drugstore?

   _____.

4. _____?

   It's usually in the corner, in the back of the store.

Write sentences:

Need	**Place to go**
I need to get some shampoo.	Go to the cosmetics section.
_____.	_____ the pharmacy.
_____.	_____ stationery section.
_____ aspirin.	_____.
_____soft drinks.	_____.
_____a broom.	_____.
_____.	_____.
_____.	_____.

Lesson 6 Activity Pages

A. Look at the key. Listen and mark the correct locations.

ABC Drugstore

1 – Stationery   3 – Household goods   5 – Pharmacy   7 – Photo   9 – Liquor

2 – Cosmetics   4 – Cold Medicine   6 – Ice Cream   8 – Checkout

B. Look at the picture. Write the answers.

1. I need to buy some lipstick.

    Go to the cosmetics section. _____*It's on the right, in the back corner*_____ .

2. I'm looking for some envelopes.

    They're in the _____, on the right side of the store.

3. Where can I find the cough medicine?

    In the _____ section, in _____, on

    _____ .

4. Excuse me, where can I find a mop?

    In the _____, in _____, on

    _____ .

C. Write the items under the correct sections.

Cosmetics	Stationery	Cold Medicine
_____	_____	_____
_____	_____	_____

Household Goods	Personal Grooming	Ice Cream
_____	_____	_____
_____	_____	_____

Items

greeting cards	frozen yogurt	shampoo	popsicles
cough syrup	paper towels	soap	lipstick
aspirin	wrapping paper	perfume	frying pan

I. Listening Comprehension

Listen and circle the correct answer, A or B.

1.

    A   B

2.

    A   B

3.

    A   B

4.

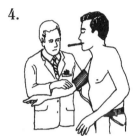 

    A   B

5.

    A   B

6.

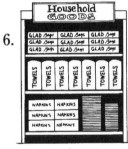 

    A   B

7.

    A   B

8.

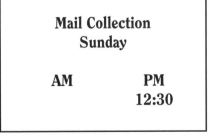

A. Yes, there is.   B. No, there isn't.

II. Reading

Circle the correct answers.

1. Betty: I'm home sick.

   Jim: _____.

   | Call home. | Go to bed. | Go to the doctor. |

2. First Class letters _____ by air.

   go   goes   send

3. You're cold! Why _____
   you put on this sweater?

   do   don't   aren't

4. The pharmacy is _____ the right.

   in   on   off

III. Writing

Write the questions or answers.

Lupe is sending an Airmail letter to her parents in El Salvador. She is putting a picture of Julio and Ana in the envelope. They are her children. She is also sending her parents a money order.

1. _____ Lupe's parents _____?

   They live in El Salvador.

2. How is she sending the letter to her parents?

   She's sending it _____.

3. What is she sending in her letter?

   _____.

4. Does her letter need an international Airmail stamp?

   _____.

Unit Three

Getting Around

Lesson 7

I Need to Go to San Francisco

Objectives: In this lesson you will learn to make airline reservations.

✔ Review: Where Are You Going?

I'm going to...

| the hardware store | the post office | the bank |

I need to get...

some nails   an Airmail stamp   some cash

I want to...

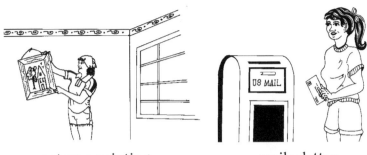

put up a painting

mail a letter

cash a paycheck

Something New: Airline Reservations
Listen and Look

a round–trip reservation for Mexico City

a one–way reservation for Seattle

the smoking section

the non–smoking section

an aisle seat

a window seat

☛ Practice Activity: Substitutions

1. I need to make a round–trip reservation for New York City.
   He   one–way
   We   round–trip   Mexico City.
   I   Chicago.

2. He'd like to sit in the smoking section.
   She wants to
   I   non–smoking section.

3. I'd like an aisle seat.
   She a window seat.
   He

Let's Talk: At the Ticket Counter

Anita wants to go to her father's wedding
next month. She needs to make airline
reservations. She's at the USA Airlines office.

Anita: I need to make a
       reservation for San
       Francisco for Friday
       the 20th of next month.

Agent: Is that a round–trip
       reservation?

Anita: Yes, it is.

Agent: When do you want
       to return?

Anita: (I'd like to return) On Sunday evening, the 22nd.

Agent: Just a minute. I'll check the available seats.

☛ Practice: "When do you need to leave?"

1. S1: Would you like a round–trip reservation?

   S2: Yes, thank you.

2. S1: Do you need a round–trip reservation?

   S2: No, one way, please.

3. S1: When do you need to leave?

   S2: (I need to leave) On Wednesday, the 5th.

4. S1: When do you want to return?

   S2: (I want to return) On the 20th.

5. S1: Do you want the smoking or non–smoking section?

   S2: (The) Non–smoking (section), please.

6. S1: Would you prefer an aisle or window seat?

   S2: I'd like an aisle seat.

☛ Practice Activity: Making Reservations

With a partner, ask and answer questions about making airline reservations.

JULY						
SUNDAY	MONDAY	TUESDAY	WEDNESDAY	THURSDAY	FRIDAY	SATURDAY
				1	2	3
4	5	6	7	8	9	10
11	12	13	14	15	16	17
18	19	20	21	22	23	24
25	26	27	28	29	30	31

Questions to ask and answer:

(Destination) Where do you need to go?

(One way or round trip) Do you need a round–trip reservation?

(Date of Departure) When do you need/want to leave?

(Date of Return) When do you want to return?

(Smoking or non–smoking section) Would you like/Do you want…?

(Aisle or window seat) Would you like/Do you want…?

Reading: At the Airport

Terminal 5 — All-Ways Airlines

What are the different areas of an airport?

Find the different areas on the diagram and discuss them.

Discussion

Anita is at the airport. She's going to San Francisco on All–Ways Airlines.

1. What terminal does she need to go to?
2. Where does she need to check her bags?
3. Where can she find out about her departure gate?
4. What is a security check?
5. Can she get something to eat before her flight? Where?
6. She wants to buy a magazine to read on the plane. Can she buy one at the airport?
7. On the diagram draw Anita's steps to get on the plane.

✍ Writing

Use the airport terminal diagram. Write the terminal areas for the activities.

1. Check your baggage at the _____.

2. Put your bags on the x–ray machine and walk through the _____.

3. Look at the _____ to find your boarding gate number.

4. Buy a magazine at the _____.

5. Go to the _____ to get a boarding pass and get on the plane.

6. Enjoy the flight!

✍✍ More Writing

1. Where do you need to go? _____ to Seattle.

2. _____ she want round–trip reservations?
   Yes, she does.

3. _____ want to leave?

4. When _____ want to return?

   He _____ on the 30th.

   I _____ on the 4th of next month.

5. Would you like smoking or non–smoking?

   _____ the non–smoking section, please.

6. Do you want an aisle seat?

   No, _____.

Lesson 7 Activity Pages

A. Listen and circle the correct information.

Fill in the departure and return dates and times as you listen.

M = morning   **A = afternoon**   **E = evening**

Speaker	Destination	Date of Departure	Time of Day	Date of Return	Time of Day
1	Seattle	Dec.	M A E	Jan.	M A E
2	San Francisco	May	M A E	May	M A E
3	Los Angeles	Oct.	M A E	Oct.	M A E
4	New York	July	M A E	July	M A E
5	London	Nov.	M A E	Dec.	M A E
6	Paris	April	M A E	April	M A E

B. Put the sentences in the correct order.

_____ Go through security.

_____ Find out your gate.

_____ Board the plane.

_____ Go to the gate.

_____ Get your boarding pass.

_____ Go to the airport early.

_____ Make a reservation.

_____ Check your bags.

_____ Enjoy your flight.

C. Ask and answer the questions with your partner.

		You		Your Partner	
1.	Is there an airport near your home?	Yes	No	Yes	No
2.	Did you fly to the U.S.?	Yes	No	Yes	No
3.	Do you like to fly?	Yes	No	Yes	No
4.	Do you go to the airport sometimes?	Yes	No	Yes	No
5.	Are you planning a flight soon?	Yes	No	Yes	No
6.	Where do you want to go in the world?	_____		_____	

Notes

The Flight Leaves at 8:45

Objectives: In this lesson you will learn how to read a flight schedule.

✔ Review: A Dream Vacation

You have two weeks of vacation.

Choose a city to visit.

Take the roles of traveler and travel agent.

Make reservations for your trip.

Something New: Reading an Airline Schedule

U.S. West Airline				
Flight	Departing to	Departure Time	Arrival Time	Gate
48	San Francisco	9:40 a.m.	10:55 a.m.	33
153	Denver	9:55 a.m.	2:00 p.m.	36
56	Houston	10:10 a.m.	2:40 p.m.	38
501	Seattle	10:30 a.m.	1:55 p.m.	37
278	Chicago	10:45 a.m.	4:10 p.m.	35

Flight 56 goes to Houston.

It leaves this city at 10:10 a.m.

It arrives in Houston at 2:40 p.m.

It leaves from Gate 38.

1. Where does Flight 153 go?
2. What time does it leave this city?
3. What time does it arrive in Denver?
4. What gate does it leave from?

☛ Practice: "What time does it leave?"

Practice with a partner. Ask and answer questions about other flights.

1. Where does…?
2. What time…leave…?
3. What time…arrive…?
4. What gate…?

Let's Talk: Flight 48

Anita is in Los Angeles. She is talking to her friend Jane. Jane is in San Francisco.

Anita: I'm taking Flight 48 on U.S. West Airlines on Friday morning.

Jane: U.S. West Airlines, Flight 48? What time does it leave?

Anita: (It leaves) At 9:40.

Jane: What time does it arrive in San Francisco?

Anita: (It arrives) At 10:55.

Jane: Great. I'll meet you at the airport.

☛ Practice: "Where does Flight 278 go?"

1. S1: Where does Flight 278 go?
   S2: It goes to Chicago.

2. S1: What time does Flight 56 leave?
   S2: It leaves at 10:10.

3. S1: What time does Flight 153 arrive in Denver?
   S2: It arrives at 2:00 p.m.

4. S1: What gate does Flight 501 leave from?
   S2: It leaves from Gate 37.

	Departure	Arrival
San Francisco	7:20 AM	9:45 AM

Flight	Departure	Arrival
309	12:10 PM	4:50 PM

5. S1: When does your plane leave New York?
   S2: It leaves at 7:20.
   S1: What time does it arrive in San Francisco?
   S2: It arrives at 9:45.

6. S1: What flight are you taking?
   S2: I'm taking Flight 309.
   S1: What time does it arrive?
   S2: It arrives at 4:50.

☛ Practice Activity: A Travel Itinerary

Anita received this travel itinerary from the travel agency.

Itinerary No. 0409071			
For: Anita Martin			
20 Sept Friday			
All–Ways Airlines	Flt: 48	Coach	Snack
Lv Los Angeles		9:40 A	
Ar San Francisco		10:55 A	
Reserved Seat 15B			
22 Sept Sunday			
All–Ways Airlines	Flt: 621	Coach	Snack
Lv San Francisco		3:30 P	
Ar Los Angeles		4:45 P	
Reserved Seat 9D			

Discussion

1. Who is traveling?
2. Where is she going?
3. What airline is she taking?
4. When is she leaving? What flight is it?
5. When is she returning? What flight is it?
6. What other information is on the itinerary?

Reading: Traveling

Sonia Mejia lives in Chicago. She is going to Miami on her vacation. She is taking Flight 305 on Southern Airlines. Flight 305 leaves Chicago at 3:20 p.m. It arrives in Miami at 7:55 p.m. Flight 305 leaves from Gate 48.

It is 2:30, and Sonia is at the airport. She is checking in at the ticket counter. She has two bags to check in, and she is getting two baggage claim checks and her boarding pass. Now she needs to go to Gate 48.

Discussion

It's 2:30 and Flight 305 leaves at 3:20. Why is Sonia at the airport early?

✍ **Writing**

1. Where does Sonia live? _____

2. Where is she going? _____

3. What flight is she taking? _____

4. What times does Flight 305 leave Chicago? _____

5. What time _____ in Miami? _____

6. What gate does it leave from? _____

7. Does Sonia have any baggage? _____

8. Is she getting a boarding pass from the airline clerk? _____

9. Where does Sonia need to go now? _____

A. *Listen to the airport announcement. Circle the correct information.*

1. Gate 54   Gate 504
2. Gate 30   Gate 13
3. Flight 17   Flight 70
4. Flight 40   Flight 414
5. 10:20   10:30
6. 5 minutes   30 minutes

B. *Talk with your partner.*

Partner A look at this page. Partner B look at E on page 75.

Ask and answer questions about the missing information. Write in the information.

North–South Airlines

Departures

Flight	Destination	Departure Time	Gate
98	Seattle	8:10 a.m.	84
17	_____	_____	_____
15	Chicago	12:00 noon	11
714	San Francisco	1:30 p.m.	10B
45	_____	_____	_____

C. *Look at the completed flight schedule and answer the questions.*

1. Where does Flight 17 go? _____

2. What time does Flight 45 leave? _____

3. What gate does Flight 45 leave from? _____

D. Match the questions to the answers.

1. Did you have a good flight?

2. What flight are you on?

3. What time does Flight 21 arrive?

4. Do you have your ticket?

5. What gate does Flight 21 leave from?

6. What time does Flight 21 leave?

_____ a. It leaves at 5:55 p.m.

_____ b. It leaves from Gate 36.

_____ c. It arrives at 8:20 a.m.

_____ d. I'm on Flight 21 to Tokyo.

_____ e. Yes, I do.

_____ f. Yes, I did.

E. Talk with your partner.

Partner B look at this page. Partner A look at page B on page 74.

Ask and answer questions about the missing information. Write in the information.

Flight	Destination	Departure Time	Gate
98	Seattle	8:10 a.m.	84
17	New York	10:30 a.m.	12
15	_____	_____	_____
714	_____	_____	_____
45	Dallas	2:20 p.m.	15A

F. Look at the completed flight schedule and write questions.

1. _____
   It leaves at 12 noon.

2. _____
   It goes to San Francisco.

3. _____
   It leaves from Gate 10B.

What Do You Have to Do?

Objectives: In this lesson you will talk about things you need to do.

✔ Review: A Plane Trip

Imagine you are taking a plane trip.

Tell your partner about your flight:

    Destination

    Flight number

    Time of departure

    Time of arrival

Something New: Things to Do
Look and Listen

Sara and Tomas are going to Honolulu on vacation.

They need to do many things before the trip.

Two weeks before the trip:

Sara has to pick up the tickets.

Tomas has to buy swimming trunks.

Sara has to buy a bathing suit.

The day before the trip:

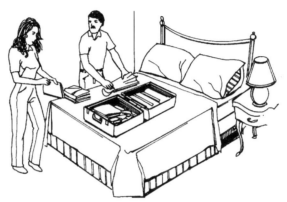

Sara and Tomas have to pack.

Let's Talk: Can You Take Us to the Airport?

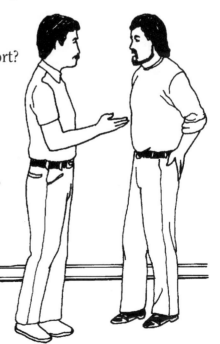

Tomas: Can you take Sara and me to the airport?

Tony: Sure. When do you want to leave?

Tomas: It takes 45 minutes to get to the airport. Can you pick us up at 9:30?

Tony: Okay. What time does the plane leave?

Tomas: At 11:30. But we have to check in an hour before the flight.

☛ **Practice: "When do you have to check in?"**

1. S1: Can you take me to the airport?
   S2: Of course. When do you have to leave?
   S1: (I have to leave) At 10:45.

2. S1: When do you have to check in?
   S2: We have to check in two hours before the flight.

3. S1: What does she have to do?
   S2: She has to pick up the tickets.

4. S1: What does he have to do?
   S2: He has to buy swim trunks.

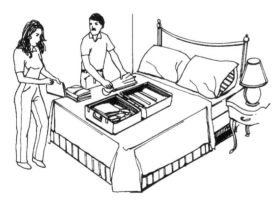

5. S1: Do you have to pack for your trip?
   S2: Yes, I do.

6. S1: Does she have to pick up the tickets?
   S2: Yes, she does.

☞ Practice: "What do you have to do today?"

1. S1: What does he have to do today?
   S2: He has to go to the post office.

2. S1: What do they have to do today?
   S2: They have to go to the market.

3. S1: What does he have to do tomorrow?
   S2: He has to wash the car.

4. S1: What do you have to do tomorrow?
   S2: I have to go to the laundromat.

☞ Practice Activity: Things to Do Today

1. Make a list of things you have to do today.
2. Share your list in a small group.
3. Tell the class what everyone in your group has to do today.

Things to Do Today

1. _____

2. _____

3. _____

4. _____

5. _____

✍ Writing

Write sentences about what the people in your group have to do today.

1. _____

2. _____

3. _____

4. _____

5. _____

★ Something Extra: Planning a Party

It's time for a party!

    What do we have to do?

    We have to _____.

Make a list of things to do for the party.

Things to Do

_____

_____

_____

_____

_____

_____

_____

Reading: Getting Ready for a Vacation

Mr. and Mrs. Johnson are going to Hawaii on vacation. They are getting ready for the trip.

Mrs. Johnson has to pick up her dress at the cleaners. She has to ask her neighbor to take care of the cat, and she has to call the newspaper to stop delivery for a week.

Mr. Johnson has to water the garden and grass before they leave. He has to go to the bank. He needs to buy travelers' checks.

Mr. and Mrs. Johnson are very busy now. There are so many things to do before their trip. But when they get to Hawaii, they can just relax!

✎ **Writing**

1. Does Mrs. Johnson have to pick up her dress at the cleaners? _____.

2. What else does she have to do?

    _____

    _____.

3. _____ Mr. Johnson _____ water the garden and grass? Yes, he does.

4. _____?

    He has to go to the bank.

5. Turn to page 82 and make a list of all the things Mr. and Mrs. Johnson have to do before their trip. Think of more things to do and add them to the list.

Make a list for Mrs. Johnson.

Things to Do

_____

_____

_____

_____

_____

_____

_____

Make a list for Mr. Johnson.

Things to Do

_____

_____

_____

_____

_____

_____

_____

A. *Match the sentences.*

Martha is complaining to her mom. Her mom is giving her advice.

1. Mom, my apartment is a mess!

2. I'm not doing well in school!

3. My friends never call me!

4. I don't have any money!

5. My hair looks terrible!

6. I'm tired all the time!

7. I'm always late for school!

8. I don't have anything to wear!

9. I'm never happy!

_____ a. You have to go to bed early!

_____ b. You have to smile more!

_____ c. You have to get a haircut!

_____ d. You have to do some laundry!

_____ e. You have to get there on time!

___1__ f. You have to clean it!

_____ g. You have to call them!

_____ h. You have to get a part–time job!

_____ i. You have to study!

B. Ask and answer the questions with your classmates.

Ask: *Do you have to…*

When you get a "yes" answer, write the student's name in the square.

You can only write each student's name once.

When you have 4 names in a row you have BINGO!

Do you have to…?

wash the car this weekend?	study English tonight?	work at night?	wash clothes this weekend?
_____	_____	_____	_____
go to the market this weekend?	wash the kitchen floor?	water the plants in your home?	pick up children at school?
_____	_____	_____	_____
go to the bank?	do homework tonight?	get up early?	clean your home this weekend?
_____	_____	_____	_____
call your family this week?	go to bed late at night?	cook for your family?	vacuum the living room this weekend?
_____	_____	_____	_____

Unit Three Evaluation

I. Listening Comprehension

Listen and circle the correct answer, A or B.

1.

A

B

2.

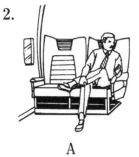

A

B

3.

Flight	Departing to
321	San Francisco
920	Denver

A. Flight 321

B. Flight 920

4.

Departure Time	Arrival Time
10:00 a.m.	11:15 a.m.

A   B

Flight	Departing to	Departure Time	Arrival Time	Gate
1232	Miami	3:15 p.m.	6:45 p.m.	81
410	Chicago	3:45 p.m.	6:10 p.m.	78

5.

A. Gate 81   B. Gate 78

6.

A. Flight 1232   B. Flight 410

7.

A

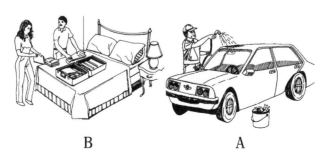

B

8.

A

B

II. Reading

Circle the correct answer.

1. She _____ to go to
   San Francisco.

   have   has   want

2. What time _____ it
   arrive in Honolulu?

   is   has   does

3. _____ you like the smoking
   or non–smoking section?

   Are   Do   Would

4. _____ prefer a window
   seat.

   I'd   He's   Yes

5. What time does Flight 510
   _____?

   go   departing   leave

6. What does she _____ to do
   today?

   have   has   having

III. Writing

Fill in the blanks with the correct words.

aisle	Chicago	has	like
non–smoking	trip	wants	

John lives in _____. He needs to go to Dallas. He needs to make a

round–_____ reservation. He _____ to leave on Friday, the

15th and return to Chicago on Saturday, the 23rd. He _____ to sit in the

_____ section. He'd _____ an _____ seat.

Unit Four

In the Past

Lesson 10

What Did He Do Last Night?

Objectives: In this lesson you will learn to talk about activities in the past.

✔ Review: What I Do Every Day

In groups of three, tell the others in your group what you do every day.

> *Examples:* Every morning I get up at _____.
>
> I have _____ for breakfast.
>
> After dinner I _____.
>
> On Saturdays I _____.

Ask and answer questions about what people in the group do every day.

Something New: What Was the Date Last Friday?

Last Week/This Week							
	Sun.	Mon.	Tue.	Wed.	Thurs.	Fri.	Sat.
Last week							
This week							

1. Write in the dates for last week and this week.
2. Circle today's date.
3. What was the date last Monday? Last Wednesday? Last Saturday?
4. What were the dates last weekend?

Something New: What Did You Do Last Week?
Listen and Look

Last Friday

Peter washed his car.

Olga studied.

Then they played cards.

On Saturday

Ben cleaned the yard.

Sue vacuumed.

Then they visited friends.

Last night

They washed the dishes.

He watched TV.

She sewed.

☛ **Practice: "Did she wash the dishes?"**

1. S1: Did he clean the yard on Friday?
   S2: Yes, he did.

2. S1: Did she watch TV last night?
   S2: No, she didn't.

3. S1: What did you do on Saturday?
   S2: I visited friends.

4. S1: What did she do yesterday?
   S2: She sewed.

Let's Talk: Did You Practice English Last Night?

Tami: Did you practice English last night?

Paul: No, I didn't, but I learned some
new words in English.

Tami: What did you do?

Paul: I watched a movie on TV.

☛ Practice Activity: Substitutions

1. I watched TV.
   He
   They
      visited friends.
   She
   We played cards.
         soccer.

2. Did you clean the yard yesterday?
      he
            wash the car last Saturday?
      she
            play baseball last weekend?
      they

3. What did you do last night?
                  yesterday?
      they
                  last weekend?
      she
                  this morning?

☛ Practice Activity: What did they do in the evening?

bake   work   play cards

Tell about Mr. and Mrs. Garcia's day last Saturday.

1. What did Mrs. Garcia do in the morning?
2. What did Mr. Garcia do all day?
3. What did they do in the evening?

play tennis

vacuum

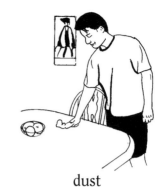

dust

Tell about Henry Sato's day yesterday.

1. Did Henry Sato wash his car yesterday?

2. What did he do?

mow

watch TV

play soccer

Tell about Bill Martin's day last Sunday.

1. What did Bill do last Sunday?

2. What do you think he usually does on Sunday?

■ Interaction: What Did You Do Last Weekend?

Ask four people about their past weekend. Ask them if they played baseball, played soccer, washed the car, rented a video, cleaned the house, watched TV, washed clothes, visited friends, etc. on Saturday or Sunday.

Name	Activities	Saturday/Sunday

Reading: The Martin Family's Weekend

The Martin family stayed at home last Saturday. Pat vacuumed the house and mopped the kitchen. Paul cleaned the yard. He mowed the lawn, raked the grass, and weeded the garden. John and Luisa helped him.

In the afternoon Paul worked on his car and Pat sewed. The children played outside with their friends.

In the evening the family rented two videos. John and Luisa watched a cartoon. Then Paul and Pat watched a comedy.

✍ Writing

1. Did the Martin family stay at home last Saturday? _____.

2. What did Pat do?

   _____.

3. _____?

   He cleaned the yard.

4. What did Paul do in the afternoon?

   _____.

5. _____?

   They played outside with their friends.

6. Did the Martins play cards in the evening? _____.

7. What did they do?

   _____.

Lesson 10 Activity Pages

A. Listen to Charlie's day and number the pictures.

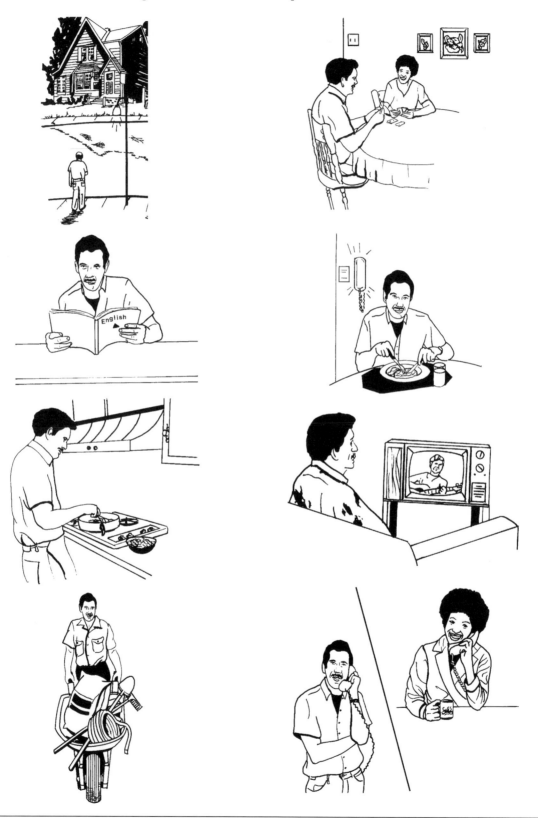

B. Write the missing words in Charlie's story.

answered	cleaned	cooked	invited	played	rested
started	studied	talked	visited	walked	watched

Last Sunday was very nice! Charlie _____*cleaned*_____ he yard in the afternoon.

Then he _____ in the living room and _____

TV. He _____ English for an hour before dinner. At 6:00 he

_____ a delicious dinner: salad, chicken and rice. He

_____ to eat when the phone started to ring. He

_____ the phone and _____ to his

friend, Michelle. Michelle _____ Charlie to her house. Charlie

_____ to Michelle's house at 7:30. The friends _____

for an hour and then they _____ cards.

Unit Four | Lesson 11

What School Did He Attend?

Objectives: In this lesson you will talk about schools for children.

✔ Review: Last Week

Talk to three students. Ask each student three or four questions.

Examples: What did you do last week?
Did you play _____ last week?
Did you learn _____ last week?
Did you wash _____ last week?
Did you visit _____ last week?

Something New: U.S. Schools
Listen and Look

Henry Kim is 5 years old.
He's in kindergarten.
He attends elementary school.

Bill Soto is 10 years old.
He's in 5th grade.
He attends elementary school.

Alice Mota is 12 years old.
She's in 7th grade.
She attends Oakwood Middle School.

Olga Pulanski is 16 years old.
She's a junior. (She's in 11th grade.)
She attends Washington High School.

Let's Talk: He Graduated in June

Bill is asking Ken about his son, Peter.

Bill: I don't see Peter around any more. Does he still attend high school?

Ken: Oh, no. He graduated in June. He attends college in Eastwood now.

Bill: That's a very good school, and it's expensive, too!

Ken: We're lucky. He received a scholarship. It pays his tuition.

☛ Practice: "What grade is he in?"

1. S1: What elementary school did Bill attend?

   S2: He attended Chapman Street School.

2. S1: What junior high school did he attend?

   S2: He attended Oakwood Middle School.

3. S1: What high school did he attend?

   S2: He attended Washington High (School).

4. S1: When did he graduate?

   S2: He graduated in June.

5. S1: What grade is he in?

   S2: He's in fifth grade.

   S1: What school does he attend?

   S2: He attends Chapman Street School.

6. S1: What grade is she in?

   S2: She's in eleventh grade.

   S1: Did she attend a middle school before high school?

   S2: No, she attended a junior high school.

☛ Practice Activity: Talking about School

Practice talking to a partner about your schools. Ask and answer questions about elementary school, middle school (junior high), and high school.

Examples: Where did you attend _____ school?

How many years did you attend _____ school? Etc.

★ Something Extra: Pronunciation of the Past Tense

1	2	3
/t/	/d/	/ɪd/
washed	cleaned	visited
He washed the car.	She cleaned the yard.	They visited friends.

What sound of the past tense is it: 1, 2, or 3?

stayed	They stayed at home.	_____
helped	She helped her father.	_____
rented	They rented a video.	_____

Listen to the teacher. Write the number of the sound of the past tense you hear.

1.	3.	5.	7.
2.	4.	6.	8.

☛ Practice Activity: Actions

What directions can you give and follow in the classroom? Use the following words:

open	close	pick up	turn on/off	touch	point

1. Give and follow the instructions. Then ask and answer *What did you do?*

    Example: S1: Open the door. What did you do?

    S2: I opened the door. Pick up your book. What did you do?

    S1: I picked up my book. Etc.

2. Report to the class on the actions you and your partner did.

3. Write sentences for some of the actions you or your partner did.

    _____

    _____

    _____

    _____

Reading: Schools in the United States

Children in the United States attend school for 13 years. Elementary school is from kindergarten through grade 5 or 6. Kindergarten is for 5–year–old children. It is the year before the first grade.

Middle school is from grades 6 through 8. Some communities have junior high school, from grades 7 through 9.

High school is from grades 9 through 12, or from grades 10 through 12.

Discussion

1. How many levels of school are there for children in the United States? What are they?
2. How old are children when they start middle school? junior high? high school?
3. How old are they when they graduate from high school?
4. Do you have kindergarten classes in your country?
5. What are the levels of school in your country?

✍ **Writing**

Write about the schools you attended.

What elementary school did you attend?

What junior high/high school did you attend?

When did you graduate?

_____

_____

_____

_____

_____

_____

_____

_____

A. *Read and listen to the verbs. Make a check under the sound you hear.*

	/t/	/d/	/ɪd/		/t/	/d/	/ɪd/
1. played				7. walked			
2. needed				8. shopped			
3. watched				9. called			
4. cleaned				10. visited			
5. showed				11. stopped			
6. missed				12. looked			

B. *Talk about the chart with your partner.*

Ask and answer the questions.

Did _____ finish the 8th grade?

Did _____ graduate from high school?

Did _____ graduate from college?

Did _____ study English in his/her country?

Did _____ study English last year?

Name	Country	Education	English
Martin	Guatemala	Finished 8th grade	Level 1A and 1B
Feliz	Turkey	Graduated from high school	1 year in Turkey; 1A and 1B in the U.S.
Liseth	El Salvador	Graduated from college	1B in the U.S.

C. Answer the questions and then compare your answers to your partner's.

1. Did you finish the 8th grade in your country? _____

2. Did you study United States' history in your country? _____

3. Did you study English in your country? _____

4. Did you study English last year? _____

5. Did you practice speaking English yesterday? _____

D. Ask and answer the questions with your classmates.

Ask: Did you _____ yesterday?

When you get a "yes" answer, write the student's name in the square.
You can only write each student's name once.
When you have 3 names in a row you have TIC TAC TOE!

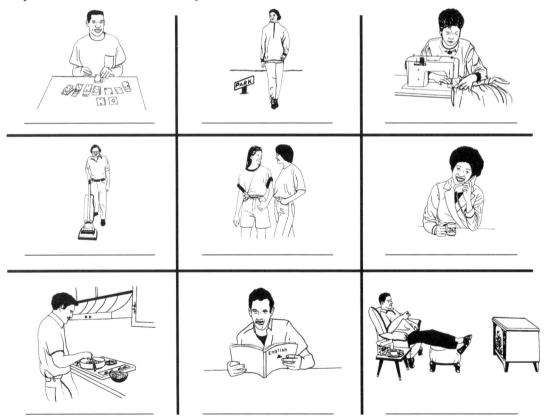

E. Use the names and the information to write about the people in class.

1. Who played cards?

   Martha played cards.

2. Who watched TV?

   _____

3. Who walked in the park?

   _____

4. Who cooked?

   _____

5. Who visited a friend?

   _____

6. Who called someone on the phone?

   _____

7. Who sewed something?

   _____

8. Who cleaned house?

   _____

9. Who studied English?

   _____

10. Who played cards?

   _____

Lesson 12

Learning Never Ends

Objectives: In this lesson you will talk about schools for adults.

✔ Review

Neighborhood Children

Talk about these children.

Tell what school they attend and what school(s) they attended before.

Tell what grade they are in.

Ask and answer questions about the children.

Li An Hoang	Yuri Orlov	Ali Hassan
7 years old	12 years old	16 years old
Amestoy School	Harris Junior High	Monroe High

What did you do last night?

Interview four classmates.

Ask questions about their activities last night.

Fill in the grid.

	Did you _____ ?					
Name	**Stay at home?**		**Wash dishes?**		**Watch TV?**		**What programs?**
	Yes	No	Yes	No	Yes	No	

Something New: Job Plans

She studied nursing
at a community college.

I studied welding
at an occupational center.

He studied television repair
at a vocational school.

They studied English
at an adult school.

Let's Talk: Did You Complete the Course?

Lenore just graduated from a vocational nursing school. She is looking for a good job. She is talking to an employment counselor.

Counselor: Do you have a vocational nursing license?

Lenore: Yes, I do. I studied nursing at a community college.

Counselor: Did you complete the course?

Lenore: Yes, I completed it in May. Then I passed the state examination and received my license.

Discussion

1. Where did Lenore study nursing?
2. When did she graduate?
3. Did she pass the state examination?
4. What did she receive after the examination?
5. Did you study for a job in your country? Did you graduate?

☛ Practice: "Did he receive his license?"

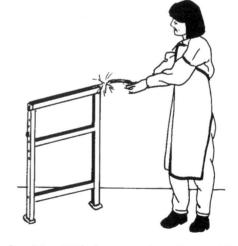

1. S1: Did he complete the TV repair course?
   S2: Yes, he did.

2. S1: Did she complete the welding course?
   S2: Yes, she did.

3. S1: Did you pass the state examination?
   S2: Yes, I did.

4. S1: Did he receive his license?
   S2: Yes, he did.

5. S1: What did he study at the community college?
   S2: He studied welding.
   S1: Did he complete the course?
   S2: Yes, he did.
   S1: Did he pass the examination?
   S2: Yes, he did. He received his license last month.

★ Something Extra: Planning for the Future

I want to be an X–ray technician.

I want to be a data processor.

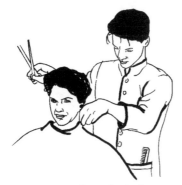

He wants to be a hairdresser.

She wants to be a caterer.

Let's Talk: I Want to Be . . .

Ted is getting his high school diploma at Westside Adult School. He is talking to the counselor about his career plans.

Counselor: What are your plans for the future, Ted?

Ted: I want to be an X–ray technician.

Counselor: They offer classes for X–ray technicians at the community college. It's a two–year program.

Ted: Thank you for telling me.

☛ Practice Activity: Career Plans

Talk to your partner about your career plans. Ask and answer:
1. What are your plans for the future?
2. What do you want to be?
3. What kind of training do you need?

Reading: It's Never Too Late

Why do adults go to school? Some go to school because it is fun. They want to learn photography, painting, or to play the guitar.

Many people go to school to learn new skills. Schools offer education, and they also offer training for many different kinds of occupations.

By going to school people get promotions and raises, and many get better jobs, too.

Discussion

1. Why do adults go to school?
2. Why do you want to learn English?
3. Do you know someone who now works in a better job because of going to school? Tell about the person.

✍️ Writing

1. What does she want to be?

_____

_____

2. Where did he study welding?

_____

_____

3. Did he complete the course?

_____

4. _____ the

state examination?

Yes, I did.

Fill in the blanks:

Wilma Polsky wants to _____ a data processor. She _____

data processing at a community college. She _____ the course last month.

She _____ the final examination. She _____ a certificate

from the college. Now she is looking for a good job.

Lesson 12 Activity Pages

A. Fill out the form with your education and experience.

Circle the highest grade completed.

1 2 3 4 5 6 7 8 9 10 11 12 13 14 15 16

1. Did you study at a vocational school?

_____

2. What did you study?

_____

3. Did you study at a university or college?

_____

4. What did you study?

_____

5. Did you study English in your country?

_____

6. Did you work in your country?

_____

7. What was your job?

_____

8. Where do you want to work?

_____

9. What do you want to do?

_____

B. Make questions from the statements.

Write the questions first.
Ask and answer the questions with your classmates.
Write the names of your classmates who answer "yes" on the correct lines.

1. Find someone who watched TV last night.

    Did you watch TV last night? _____ 1. _____

2. Find someone who rented an apartment last year.

    _____ 2. _____

3. Find someone who finished a technical course.

    _____ 3. _____

4. Find someone who studied English in their country.

    _____ 4. _____

5. Find someone who looked for a job last week.

    _____ 5. _____

6. Find someone who applied for a job last week.

    _____ 6. _____

7. Find someone who learned English from TV.

    _____ 7. _____

8. Find someone who graduated from college.

    _____ 8. _____

Notes

Unit Four

I. Listening Comprehension

Listen and circle the correct answer, A or B.

1.

     A   B

2.

     A   B

3.

     A   B

4.

     A   B

5.

     A   B

6.

A. No, she doesn't.
B. No, she didn't.

7.   **/t/**   **/d/**   **8.**   **/d/**   **/ɪd/**

     A   B   A   B

II. Reading

Circle the correct answer.

1. Tony _____ tennis last Sunday.

   plays   played   playing

2. Mrs. Garcia baked a cake _____.

   this morning   every day   tomorrow

3. _____ you study English last night?

   Are   Do   Did

4. They visited friends _____ Saturday.

   next   every   last

5. She _____ from a community college in June.

   graduated   completed   passed

6. He's seven years old. He is in _____ school.

   junior high   elementary   high

III. Writing

Fill in the blanks.

1. What course did you study?

   _____ nursing.

   _____ you finish your studies?

   Yes, _____.

   _____ you _____ the state examination?

   Yes, I did. I _____ my state license in July.

2. What _____ your daughter want to be?

   She _____ a data processor.

Unit Five

Places to Go, Things to Do

What Did You Do Last Sunday?

Objectives: In this lesson you will talk about past weekend activities.

✔ Review: Every Week; Last Week

1. What do you do every week? Did you do the activity last week?
2. What do you do every Friday? Did you do the activity on Friday?
3. What do you do every month? Did you do the activity last month?

Something New: Places to Go for Fun
Listen and Look

We went to the park yesterday.

The children went to the zoo on Sunday.

They went to the carnival last night.

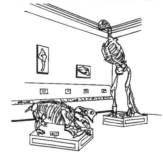

I went to the museum last week.

She went to the swap meet on Saturday.

We went to the movies last month.

☛ **Practice: "Where did you go?"**

1. S1: Where did you go last Sunday?
   S2: I went to the zoo.

2. S1: Where did he go last night?
   S2: He went to the carnival.

Let's Talk: We Went to the Ball Park

It's Monday. Ricardo Soto is talking with Don Kim at work.

Don: Where did you go yesterday?

Ricardo: I went to the ball park.

The Dodgers played the Chicago Cubs.

Don: Did your family go with you?

Ricardo: Yes. The children didn't watch the game very much, but they enjoyed the hot dogs and peanuts.

☛ **Practice: "Did Ann and Mark go with you?"**

1. S1: Did Ann and Mark go with you?
   S2: No, they didn't.
   S1: Where did they go?
   S2: They went to the museum.

2. S1: Where did Mario go on Sunday?
   S2: He went to the park.
   S1: Did his family go with him?
   S2: Yes, they did.

Something New: What Did You See?
Listen and Look

We saw elephants at the zoo.

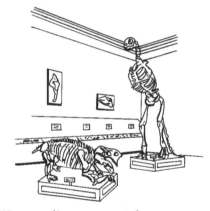

We saw dinosaurs at the museum.

I saw "The Beautiful Mermaid" at the movies.

She saw some jewelry at the swap meet.

☞ Practice: "We saw dinosaurs"

1. S1: Where did you go yesterday?

   S2: We went to the museum.

   S1: What did you see there?

   S2: We saw dinosaur fossils.

2. S1: Where did they go last Sunday?

   S2: They went to the zoo.

   S1: What did they see?

   S2: They saw elephants.

3. S1: Did you see some old books at the swap meet?

   S2: Yes, I did. Lots of them.

4. S1: Did you see the ball game yesterday?

   S2: Yes, we did. We watched it on TV.

★ Something Extra: More Weekend Activities

We went to the circus and saw the clowns.

She went to the art museum and saw many paintings.

They went to the lake and saw some boats.

He went to the aquarium and saw a lot of fish.

☞ Practice: "Where did you go?"

Can you think of some more places to go for fun? Practice with a partner.

S1: Where did you go on _____?

S2: I went to _____.

S1: What did you see there?

S2: I saw _____.

☞ Practice: "What did you see?"

1. S1: Did you see dinosaurs at the art museum?

   S2: No, I didn't.

   S1: What did you see?

   S2: I saw paintings.

2. S1: Did he see boats at the aquarium?

   S2: No, he didn't.

   S1: What did he see?

   S2: He saw a lot of fish.

☞ Practice Activity: Where did you go?

1. Discuss places to visit in your groups. Ask who went someplace in the past.
2. Ask where they went and what they saw. Write the answers below.

	Name	Where	When	What
1.	Tony	ball park	last Sunday	ball game
2.				
3.				
4.				
5.				

Reading: Amusement Parks

Children and adults love amusement parks, big or small. There are many big parks around the country. In California, there is Disneyland, and in Texas you can visit Six Flags. In Florida, Disney World and Epcot Center are waiting for you.

There are small carnivals that move from city to city. Overnight an empty lot on the corner can become a gay carnival. In a couple of days the carnival moves on to another city.

You can find all kinds of rides and games at the big parks. You can see the roller coaster and the ferris wheel from miles away. You can hear the music and the people's shouts, too.

Discussion

1. Is there an amusement park near your home?
2. Do you know about Disneyland or Six Flags?
3. Are amusement parks expensive?
4. Do small carnivals come to your city?
5. What is your favorite ride?

✍ Writing

Fill in the blanks.

Don: _____ you _____ last weekend?

Jim: _____ to the movies.

Don: _____ your family _____, too?

Jim: Yes, _____.

Don: What movie _____ you _____?

Jim: We _____ "The Beautiful Mermaid."

✏️✏️ More Writing

Write a short note to a friend or relative in another city. Write about a place you visited last weekend or last month and what you saw there.

Use correct letter writing form:

    Write the date in the upper right corner.

    Write the salutation: Dear _____,

    Write the closing: Sincerely, or _____,

    Sign your letter.

Lesson 13 Activity Page

A. Listen to Rosa talk about where she went last Saturday.

Follow her route with your pencil.

Now listen to Rosa again and circle what she saw at each place she went.

B. Ask and answer the questions with your partner.

	You	Your Partner
1. Where did you go on Sunday?	_____	_____
2. Did you go with your family?	_____	_____
3. Did you go to work yesterday?	_____	_____
4. When did you last go to the movies?	_____	_____
5. What movie did you see?	_____	_____
6. When did you last have fun?	_____	_____
7. Where did you go?	_____	_____
8. What did you see?	_____	_____

How Was the Weather?

Objectives: In this lesson you will learn to discuss the weather.

✔ Review: Fun Outings

Where did you go yesterday/last Sunday/last week?

1. Talk about your past fun activities.
2. List the names of the students and their activities on the board: Where they went and what they saw.

Something New: How Was the Weather?

Listen and Look

It's cloudy.

It's sunny.

It's windy.

It's calm.

It's foggy.

It's clear.

It's rainy.

It's snowy.

☞ Practice: "It's windy"

1. S1: How's the weather?
   S2: It's windy today.

2. S1: Is it a rainy day?
   S2: Yes, and it's windy, too.

Let's Talk: Where Were You Last Weekend?

Sue: Where were you last weekend?
     I called you several times.

May: I was in San Francisco for a wedding.

Sue: Really?

May: Yes. It was a beautiful outdoor wedding.

Sue: In San Francisco? How was the weather?

May: It was foggy in the morning, but sunny
     and clear in the afternoon.

☛ Practice: "I was at the movies"

1. S1: Where were you yesterday?
   S2: I was at the movies.

2. S1: Where was Ben last Friday?
   S2: He was at the ball park.

3. S1: Where were you last week?
   S2: We were in San Diego.
   S1: How was the weather?
   S2: It was sunny and warm.

4. S1: Where were you last Sunday?
   S2: I was at the lake.
   S1: How was the weather?
   S2: It was rainy.

5. S1: Was Tom at the wedding?
   S2: Yes, he was.
   S1: Was his wife there, too?
   S2: Yes, she was.

6. S1: Were they at the party?
   S2: No, they weren't.
   S1: Where were they?
   S2: They were in San Francisco.

☛ Practice Activity: How was the weather?

Discuss the weather in various cities.

> ***Example:*** S1: Where were you last month?
> S2: I was in _____.
> S1: How was the weather there?
> S2: It was _____.

☛ Practice Activity: Weather around the World

In the U.S. we say, "Everyone talks about the weather, but no one does anything about it."

Is this true in your country, too? Is weather a favorite topic of conversation?

Talk about the weather in your native countries and make a chart.

Some questions to ask:

　　1. How many seasons do you have in your country? What are they?

　　2. What are your summer months and winter months?

　　3. Are your summers very hot and your winters very cold?

　　4. What city do you think has the best weather?

Name	City or Country	Weather
Kinu	Tokyo	hot summers, cold winters

Reading: The Weather Report

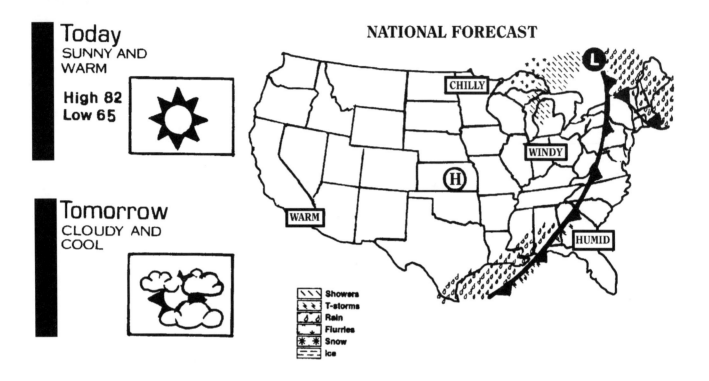

TODAY'S WEATHER

Today
SUNNY AND WARM

High 82
Low 65

Tomorrow
CLOUDY AND COOL

NATIONAL FORECAST

CHILLY
WINDY
WARM
HUMID

Showers
T-storms
Rain
Flurries
Snow
Ice

What's the weather today? Did you read the weather report in the newspaper? Did you watch it on TV?

Do I need to take my umbrella to work? What's the temperature today? Do I need a sweater or a jacket? The weather report can answer these questions for us.

But sometimes the weatherman's report is wrong. Then we are in trouble.

Discussion

1. Do you follow the weather report in the newspaper or on TV?
2. Does the weather change very much in your city?
3. Which are the nicest months of the year?

✍ Writing

1. Where did you go last week?

   _____to London.

   How _____ the weather there?

   _____.

2. _____ Bill _____ last week?

   _____ to Cancun.

   How was the weather in Cancun?

   _____.

✍✍ More Writing

Write a weather report about yesterday's weather, and then write a report about today's weather.

In your reports write about the temperature (mild, warm, hot, cold, chilly, etc.) as well as the weather (foggy, cloudy, rainy, etc.).

Lesson 14 Activity Pages

A. *Look at the pictures.*

Listen to the report and circle the correct letter.

1.

a   b   c

2.

a   b   c

3.

a   b   c

4.   a   b   c

5.   a   b   c.

B. Look at this page, and your partner looks at E on page 133.

Ask and answer the questions about the people below. Write in the missing information.

Name	Where does _____ live?	Where did ____ go on Saturday?	What did _____ see?	How was the weather?
Gary	Cleveland	*art museum*	*paintings*	rainy
Emily	Portland	zoo	animals	_____
Dave	_____	_____	_____	sunny
Anna	_____	movies	an action movie	_____
Lourdes	New York	_____	_____	cloudy

C. Look at the information in B or E. Write the questions and answers.

1. Where did Gary go last Saturday?

   *He went to the art museum.*_____

2. How was the weather in Cleveland last Saturday?

   It _____.

3. _____?

   It was cloudy.

4. Where did Emily go?

   _____.

5 What did Lourdes see at the park?

   _____.

D. Look at the postcard from Sara to her friend.

Write the correct words in the blanks.

am	didn't	from	in
is	to	was	went

Dear Micko,

How are you? I have a cold. The weather _____ Los Angeles

is usually beautiful, but it _____ very rainy and windy now. I

_____ to an outdoor wedding yesterday, but I _____

have my umbrella. It _____ a beautiful wedding, but terrible

weather. I think that is why I _____ sick now. Please write

soon. I need _____ get a letter _____ you!

Love, Sara

Micko Suzuki
78 E. 57th St. #4
N.Y., NY 10016

E. Look at this page, and your partner looks at B on page 131.

Ask and answer the questions about the people below:

Name	Where does _____ live?	Where did ___ go on Saturday?	What did _____ see?	How was the weather?
Gary	*Cleveland*	art museum	paintings	*rainy*
Emily	_____	_____	_____	windy
Dave	Las Vegas	flea market	books	_____
Anna	Berkeley	_____	_____	foggy
Lourdes	_____	a park	a concert	_____

Lesson 15

Places to Visit in the U.S.

Objectives: In this lesson you will talk about some famous places in the U.S.

✔ Review: Talking about the Weather

Write a weather report for today on the board and discuss it. What is the forecast for tomorrow? What do you think?

Something New: The United States

Discussion

1. Look at the map of the United States. Find your state on the map and write its name on it.
2. Point to the regions of the U.S.: the East, West, Midwest, and South.
3. Find some important cities: the capital city, San Francisco, New York City, etc.
4. Find some famous national parks: Yosemite, Yellowstone, Grand Canyon.

Something New: U.S. Landmarks

I went to San Francisco on my vacation.

She went to New York City on her vacation.

He went to Yellowstone National Park on his vacation.

We went to Yosemite National Park on our vacation.

They went to Washington, D.C. on their vacation.

We went to the Grand Canyon on our vacation.

☞ Practice: "They went to the Grand Canyon"

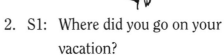

1. S1: Where did they go on their vacation?
   S2: They went to Yosemite National Park.
   S1: Where is Yosemite?
   S2: It's in California.

2. S1: Where did you go on your vacation?
   S2: We went to the Grand Canyon.
   S1: Where is it?
   S2: It's in Arizona.

★ Something Extra: What Did You Do There?

They saw the famous Yosemite Falls.

He saw the White House.

We rode the cable cars.

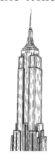

We went to the top of the
Empire State Building.

I rode a mule down into the canyon.

We went hiking. We saw
a lot of animals.

☛ Practice Activity: Guess the vacation places

1. Six students go to the front of the class with different vacation pictures. Do not show the pictures to the class.

2. Other students ask yes/no questions about their vacations. Guess their vacation places.

   Examples: Did you go east/west/north/south?

   Did you go to a city? a national park?

   Did you ride a cable car? go hiking? Etc.

☛ **Practice: "What did he do there?"**

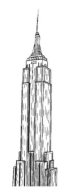

1. S1: Where did he go on his vacation?
   S2: He went to San Francisco.
   S1: What did he do there?
   S2: He rode the cable cars.

2. S1: Where did you go on your vacation?
   S2: I went to New York.
   S1: What did you do there?
   S2: I went to the top of the Empire State Building.

Reading: A School Composition

Lisa Gomez is in the sixth grade at Crest Elementary School. This is her composition for her class.

What I Did on My Summer Vacation

In July my family and I went to Washington, D.C. on our vacation. It is our nation's capital city. There are many historical buildings in the capital. They are all important to us because they tell the story of the United States. We saw the White House, the Lincoln Memorial and the Washington Monument. We visited the Capitol Building and saw the senators and congressmen and congresswomen at work.

Discussion

1. Where did Lisa and her family go on her summer vacation?
2. Can you find Washington, D.C. on the U.S. map?
3. What did Lisa's family see in Washington, D.C.?
4. What did Lisa and her family see at the Capitol Building?
5. What is the capital city of your state? of your country?
6. Where would you like to go on your vacation next year?

✍ Writing

1. They_____

_____vacation.

2. We_____

_____ vacation.

3. Where _____ she _____

_____?

She went to Washington, D.C.

4. _____ they _____

_____?

They went to Yellowstone.

★ Something Extra: Famous Places Around the World

Write about a famous place to visit in your country. What's its name? Where is it? What do people do there? When did you visit this place? What did you see and do?

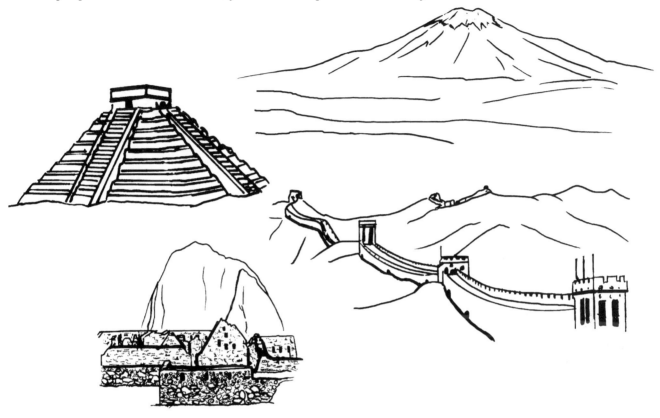

Mrs. Taylor: Every country is proud of its famous landmarks. Can you tell us about Mexico, Pedro?

Pedro: Mexico City and the pyramids are very popular. And there are wonderful beaches and fishing resorts.

Mrs. Taylor: What about China, May?

May: Everyone knows about the Great Wall, of course, as well as historical cities like Beijing.

Mrs. Taylor: And we all know about Machu Picchu in Peru and Mt. Fuji in Japan. And the Alps in Europe. The world is full of wonderful places.

Discussion

1. What are some of Mexico's landmarks?
2. What is a famous piece of Chinese history?
3. Where do tourists like to go in Peru?
4. What are some famous mountains in the world?

A. Talk about the picture.

B. Look at the picture and write the conversation.

Martin: How was your vacation, Sam?

Sam: _____.

Martin: Where did you go?

Sam: _____.

Martin: What did you see there?

Sam: _____.

Martin: How was the weather?

Sam: _____.

Martin: What a great vacation!

C. Make questions from the statements.

Write the questions first.

Ask and answer the questions with your classmates.

Write the names of your classmates who answer "yes" on the correct lines.

1. Find someone who went to New York last year.

   Did you go to New York last year?   1. _____

2. Find someone who went to Las Vegas last year.

   _____   2. _____

3. Find someone who went to San Francisco last year.

   _____   3. _____

4. Find someone who went to a party last week.

   _____   4. _____

5. Find someone who saw a good movie last weekend.

   _____   5. _____

6. Find someone who watched TV last night.

   _____   6. _____

Notes

I. Listening Comprehension

Listen and circle the correct answer, A or B.

1.
A   B

2.
A   B

3.
A   B

4.
A   B

5.
WEATHER
High 80°
Low 70°
A

WEATHER
High 50°
Low 35°
B

6.
A   B

7.
A. No, it didn't.
B. No, it wasn't.

8.
A. Yes, they did.
B. Yes, they were.

II. Reading

Circle the correct answer.

1. Where did Ben _____ yesterday?

    go   goes   went

2. They _____ a baseball game yesterday.

    see   sees   saw

3. Did you see the White House?
   No, I _____.

    can't   don't   didn't

4. We went to New York on _____ vacation.

    his   our   go

III. Writing

Write the question or answer.

The Kono family didn't go on a trip on their vacation last summer. But they went to many places in the city. On Monday they went to the zoo. They saw many animals. They saw lions, tigers and bears. They saw monkeys and elephants, too. The children liked the farm animals. There are a lot of animals at the zoo!

1. Where did the Kono family go on their vacation?

    _____.

2. Where did the Kono family go on Monday?

    _____.

3. What animals did they see at the zoo?

    _____.

4. _____ the children _____?

    They liked the farm animals.

Unit Six

On the Road

A Great Buy?

Objectives: In this lesson you will learn about different types of cars and about buying and selling a car.

✔ Review: Vacations

In a group of three or four students, ask if anyone has visited a famous vacation place in the United States. Then discuss places near your city to visit: parks, museums, amusement parks, etc. Make a list and share it with the class.

Something New: Passenger Cars

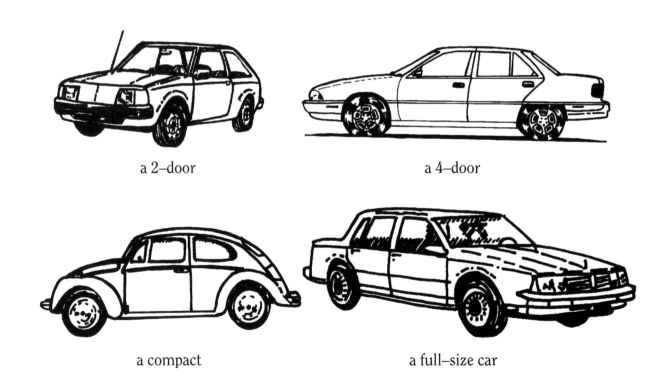

a 2–door   a 4–door

a compact   a full–size car

a station wagon

a van

a sports car

☛ Practice: "It's a 2–door"

1. S1: Do you own a car?

   S2: Yes, I do.

   S1: What kind of car is it?

   S2: It's a 2–door compact.

2. S1: Does Jack need a car?

   S2: Yes, he does.

   S1: What kind of car does he need?

   S2: He needs a station wagon, but he wants a sports car.

Something New: New or Used?

NEW — $14,000   USED — $8,000

Ricardo needs to buy a car. His 2–door compact is too small for his growing family. He wants to buy a station wagon or a van. He looked at new cars, but they are expensive. He can afford a used car.

What can he do with his old car? He can trade it in.

Discussion

1. If Ricardo gets $2,000 for a trade–in, how much more money does he have to pay for the new station wagon?

2. How much does he have to pay for the used van?

Ricardo's Car — $2,000 trade–in

Let's Talk: What Kind of Trade–in Can I Get?

Ricardo is at a used car lot, talking with a salesman.

Ricardo: I'm looking for a station wagon in good condition.

Salesman: I can show you some great buys.

Ricardo: What kind of trade–in can I get for my compact?

Salesman: I can offer you a great deal. Let me show you some cars.

☞ Practice: "I'm looking for a used car"

1. S1: Can I help you?
   S2: I'm looking for a used car.
   S1: I have some great cars in good condition.

2. S1: Can I help you?
   S2: I need a used van.
   S1: Here's a van in very good condition.

3. S1: I'd like to trade in my 4–door for a sports car.
   S2: I can give you a good price for your car.

4. S1: What kind of trade–in can I get for my car?
   S2: I can give you a good price.

■ Interaction: Trading in Cars

1. You need to trade in your old car for a newer model.
2. Find a partner to act as a salesman.
3. Talk to your partner about trading in your car.
4. Then change roles.

   Example: S1: I'd like to see some sports cars.

   S2: We have some beautiful cars.

   S1: Can I get a good trade–in for my 2–door?

   S2: Of course. I can offer you $2,000.

Something New: Buying a Used Car

Where can you look for a used car?

'88 TROJAN Cpe. Auto, air, low mileage One owner, clean $7,995	**'90 LEOPARD** Lo miles, full power, A/C and much more $12,995

1. You can find classified ads for used cars in newspapers.

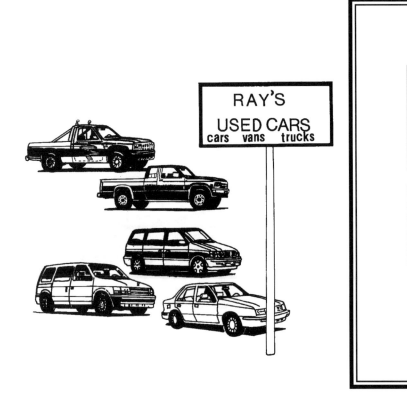

COMMUNITY BULLETIN

WANTED:
Baby sitter, days, in my home
Experienced
References required
Call: 555–7777

Room for Rent
341 Woodson Terrace
$200 a month
Call: 555–1110

For Sale
'87 Saratoga
$6,000
Call: 555–4639

RAY'S USED CARS
cars   vans   trucks

2. You can go to used car lots.   3. You can find notices at markets.

☛ Practice Activity: Ads for Cars

1. Read the following abbreviations:

A/C or air:	air conditioning
Auto:	automatic transmission
full pwr:	power steering, power brakes
lo mi:	low mileage
60K mi:	60,000 miles
xlnt cond:	excellent condition

2. Discuss the following ads in groups.

```
┌─────────────────────────┐     ┌─────────────────────────┐
│       '86 YORK          │     │      '90 MADISON        │
│ 4 dr., Auto, 65K mi., A/C,│   │     2–dr., like nu,      │
│ xlnt cond., $7,400 (white),│  │   Pwr S/B; air, AM/FM,   │
│     (818) 555–6749      │     │ black, $10,550 or best offer,│
│                         │     │  (213) 555–2197, (eves.) │
└─────────────────────────┘     └─────────────────────────┘
```

3. Tell the class which car you are interested in and why.

Reading: A Two–Car Family?

Sometimes one car is not enough for a family. Rico and Mona would like two cars, but they cannot afford them. Rico must have a car for his work. So Mona takes the bus to her job downtown. The children have a long walk to school. On rainy days, Rico drops them off on his way to work.

The family car is busy on Rico and Mona's day off. It takes them to the market for food shopping, to the mall for other shopping, and to the doctors and dentists for appointments.

Rico and Mona want to buy a good used car. They are looking at ads in the paper and notices at the market. They need to be careful when they shop for a used car. They need to follow these guidelines:

1. Compare prices.
2. Test drive the car.
3. Ask a mechanic to look over the car.

Discussion

1. Why does Rico take his car to work?
2. Where does Mona work?
3. How do the children get to school?
4. When does the family go grocery shopping?
5. Are you a two–car family?

✍ Writing

You want to sell these cars. Write classified ads for them and set the price:

1.

1988 PIONEER
4–door, air conditioning
power steering
power brakes
power locks
automatic transmission
call evenings, 555–3854,
$_____

2.

1986 SUNDANCE
2–door compact
good condition
new tires, new paint
100,000 miles
555–0758,
$_____

Fill in the blanks:

1. I'm _____ for a passenger van.

2. _____ a van in _____ condition.

3. What _____ of trade–in can I get?

4. I can _____ you a great deal.

Lesson 16 Activity Pages

A. *Listen to the people talk about their lifestyles.*

Decide what kind of car each person needs and make a check in the correct column.

	2–door	station wagon	4–door	van	compact	sports car
1. Lisa						✔
2. Ben						
3. Ricardo						
4. Carla						
5. Frances						
6. Magda						

B. *Read the advertisements and choose the car you'd like.*

1.
FOR SALE

'87 Saratoga

air, $6,000

Call 555–4639

2.
FOR SALE

'89 Honda Civic

2 dr, a/c, $4,000

Call a.m. 394–9101

3.
FOR SALE

Classic '85 Rabbit

xlnt cond. 100K

$5,000 or best offer

(818) 473–7085 eves only

4.
FOR SALE

'79 Wagon

4 dr, like nu

AM/FM/Cass, air

pwr, lo mi.

make offer (201) 788–6542

C. Ask and answer the questions about the advertisements on page 153.

1. How much is the '87 Saratoga?

   _It's $6,000_____.

2. Does it have _____?

   Yes, it does.

3. What year is the Honda Civic?

   It's an _____.

4. What car has low mileage?

   _____.

5. _____ the wagon

   have _____?

6. When can I call about the Rabbit?

   _____.

D. Write a short paragraph about the kind of car you would like to buy and why.

_____

_____

_____

_____

_____

_____

_____

Notes

We Bought It for Work and Play

Objectives: In this lesson, you will learn about different kinds of vehicles and also about public transportation.

✔ Review: Buying and Selling a Car

1. Act as a seller and a buyer to sell your own car or to buy a car.

   Examples: I want a station wagon in good condition, etc.

   I have a 2–door in good condition. I can sell it for a good price.

2. In pairs, write a classified ad to sell your car.

   Example: '87 York, 2–dr, A–C, etc.

Join another pair and try to sell your cars to each other.

Something New: Vehicles on the Road

Vehicles on the Job (Commercial)

pick–up truck

truck and trailer

delivery van

taxicab

Weekend Vehicles (Recreational)

camper

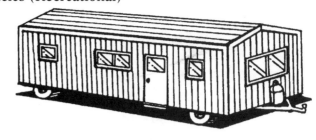

trailer

jeep

motorcycle

Let's Talk: We Bought It for Work and for Play

Victor Rivera is admiring Ken Hata's new pick–up truck.

Victor: That's a good–looking pick–up.

Ken: Thanks. We just bought it last week.

Victor: Did you buy it for work or for play?

Ken: For both. On weekends we use it for fishing.

☞ Practice: "When did you buy it?"

1. S1: When did you buy your jeep?
   S2: I bought it last week.

2. S1: When did he buy his camper?
   S2: He bought it last month.

3. S1: What did he buy?
   S2: He bought a motorcycle.
   S1: When did he buy it?
   S2: He bought it last week.

4. S1: Did he buy his pick–up for work?
   S2: Yes, he did. But he uses it on
       weekends, too.

5. S1: Is that a new camper?
   S2: Yes, it is. I bought it two weeks ago.
   S1: It looks good. Where did you buy it?
   S2: I bought it at Ben's Motors.

6. S1: Where's your compact?
   S2: I traded it in for this pick–up truck.
   S1: When did you buy it?
   S2: I bought it two weeks ago.

★ Something Extra: Public Transportation

People in large cities don't need to own a car. They can get around on buses, subways, or
light rail trains.

city bus

subway

surface light rail trains

elevated light rail trains

☞ **Practice: "How do you get to work?"**

1. S1: How do you get to work?
   S2: I take the subway.

2. S1: How does she get home?
   S2: She takes the bus.

■ Interaction: Getting Around

Two people in the group are small town residents.
Two people in the group are big city residents.

Discuss the following topics:

    1. Getting around in a big city and getting around in a small town.

    2. Why you want or don't want a car in a big city and in a small town.

    Examples: What do you like about a small town?

                  What do you like about a big city?

                  How do you get around?

                  How do you go to work?

                  Do you need a car? Why or why not?

                  Do you want a car? Why or why not?

Reading: Auto Insurance

All car owners must have auto insurance. It is the law. Auto insurance can help pay for your damages in an accident. Insurance can help pay for the other driver's costs, too. Insurance can help you if someone breaks into or steals your car. You can call your insurance agent for help with your problems.

Ken Hata needed insurance for his new pick–up. His insurance agent changed his insurance from his old station wagon to the pick–up.

Discussion

1. Why is auto insurance necessary?
2. How can it help you in an accident?
3. How can you get help from the insurance company?
4. How did Ken Hata get insurance for his new truck?
5. Some people don't have auto insurance. Do you know why?

✍ Writing

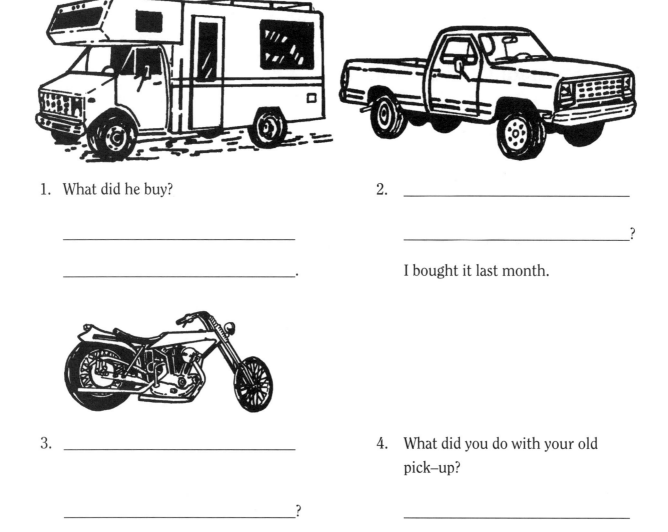

1. What did he buy?

   _____

   _____.

2. _____

   _____?

   I bought it last month.

3. _____

   _____?

   He bought it at U–Save Cycles.

4. What did you do with your old pick–up?

   _____

   _____.

Fill in the blanks.

for	in	it	on
take	There	to	two

Kim lives in New York City. Her apartment is _____

a convenient neighborhood. She can _____ the bus or the

subway _____ her job downtown. _____

is a bus stop _____ her corner. The subway station is

_____ blocks away.

A. Listen to the people talk about the vehicles they use at work and at play.

Circle the correct picture.

1.

2.

3.

4.

5.

6.

B. Make questions from the statements.

Write the questions first.
Ask and answer the questions with your classmates.
Write the names of your classmates who answer "yes" on the correct lines.

1. Find someone who has a car.

   Do you have a car?   1. _____

2. Find someone who bought a used car.

   _____   2. _____

3. Find someone who drives a motorcycle.

   _____   3. _____

4. Find someone who traded in a car.

   _____   4. _____

5. Find someone who gets to work in a pick–up truck.

   _____   5. _____

6. Find someone who went to work by bus yesterday.

   _____   6. _____

C. Talk about the picture.

D. Look at the picture and write the missing words in the story below.

bought	car	get	her	his
jeep	learning	Monday	pick–up	school
takes	waiting	work	worker	works

It's ___Monday___ morning and everybody in this picture is going to work or school.

Mrs. Jones and her daughter are _____ at the bus stop. Mrs. Jones _____

the bus to get to work, and her daughter takes it to _____ to school. Mr. Cleaver

gets to _____ on a motorcycle. He _____ his motorcycle for everyday

use. He _____ at the university and he can park it next to his office. Mr. and Mrs. Silva

bought a new _____ yesterday. Mr. and Mrs. Silva have only one _____, so

Mr. Silver drops his wife off at _____ office and then goes to _____ job. He's a

construction _____. Mrs. Simms is 75 years old but she loves her

_____. She uses it to carry her plants and groceries. She's driving it to

_____ today. She's _____ about gardening at the

occupational center. Everyone's getting around town in their own way!

Notes

Driver Occupations

Objectives: In this lesson you will learn about different types of jobs for a driver and how to interview for a job.

✔ Review: Vehicles on the Road

1. Give examples of the three types of vehicles on the road.
   Write the names on the chalkboard.

   > passenger cars
   >
   > commercial vehicles
   >
   > recreational vehicles

2. What do these vehicles carry?
   Make a list. Write the list on the chalkboard.

   > pick–ups
   >
   > trucks and trailers
   >
   > vans
   >
   > taxicabs

Something New: Driver Occupations

taxicab driver

bus driver

delivery van driver

delivery truck driver

bicycle messenger

heavy rig (semi) operator

☛ Practice: "What does he drive?"

1. S1: What does your son do?
   S2: He makes deliveries.
   S1: What does he drive?
   S2: He drives a van.

2. S1: What's your occupation?
   S2: I'm a heavy rig operator.
   S1: What do you drive?
   S2: I drive a large truck and trailer.

Let's Talk: Do You Have a Good Driving Record?

Rheza is applying for a job as a taxicab driver.

Manager: Do you have any experience as a cab driver?

Rheza: Yes, I drove a cab in Chicago for two years.

Manager: Did you have a good driving record?

Rheza: Yes, I had no traffic tickets or accidents.

Manager: How well do you know this city?

Rheza: Very well. I am driving a flower delivery truck now.

☛ Practice: "Do you have experience?"

1. S1: Do you have experience as a bus driver?

   S2: Yes. I do. I drove a bus in my country for ten years.

2. S1: What did you drive on your last job?

   S2: I drove a semi for five years.

```
COOK COUNTY SHERIFF'S DEPT.

DRIVING RECORD

NAME: JON SMITH      DATE: 3–31–94

MAY 3, 1992 – SPEEDING IN SCHOOL
ZONE IN EXCESS OF 45 MPH
FINE: $150.00          PAID 5–30–92

DEC. 19, 1991 – SPEEDING – CLOCKED
AT 55 MPH IN A 35 MPH ZONE
FINE: $100.00          PAID: 1–21–92

OCT. 7, 1991 – ACCIDENT – DRIVING
TOO FAST FOR CONDITIONS.
REAR–ENDED CAR AT STOP LIGHT.
FINE: $500.00          PAID: 10–31–91

NO OTHER RECORD OF TRAFFIC VIO-
LATIONS IN THE 36 MONTH PERIOD.

SIGNED:
Henry Ho, Sheriff
```

```
COOK COUNTY SHERIFF'S DEPT.

DRIVING RECORD

NAME: MARY JONES      DATE: 3–31–94

NO RECORD OF ANY TRAFFIC
VIOLATIONS DURING THE PAST
36 MONTHS.

SIGNED:
Henry Ho, Sheriff
```

3. S1: Did he have a good driving record?
   S2: No, he didn't. He had tickets
       and an accident on his record.

4. S1: How was her driving record?
   S2: Very good. She didn't have
       any tickets.

★ Something Extra: Auto Insurance Rates

All car owners must have auto insurance. All drivers do not pay the same rate. Drivers with traffic tickets and accidents pay high rates. Drivers with a good record pay lower rates. Drivers with new cars pay more than drivers with used cars. Sometimes sports car owners pay very high auto insurance rates.

★ Something Extra: Applying for a Job

What can help you get a job?

Job	Skills	Experience
auto mechanic	can fix cars and trucks	10 years in Mexico
chef	can cook Chinese and American food	15 years in Hong Kong
office clerk	can type and file	2 years in a school

■ Interaction: What Can You Do?

1. Draw a chart like the one below on a sheet of paper.

	Name	Job	Skills	Experience
1.				
2.				
3.				
4.				

2. Walk around the room and interview as many of your classmates as you can in 15 minutes. Fill in the information on your chart.

3. Volunteer to be an employer and call out the name of a job. See how many of your classmates have the skills and experience to apply.

Reading: Men, Women, and Jobs

Can a woman be an auto mechanic? Can she be a taxicab driver?

Little girls play house with their dolls. Little boys play with cars and trucks. Little girls grow up to be mothers and little boys become auto mechanics.

Is this always true? Times are changing. Today's little girls sometimes become mothers and wage earners. Some become bus drivers, some taxicab drivers, and some even auto mechanics. Today many families need two incomes. Many people also like to work in non–traditional jobs.

Discussion

1. What were your favorite toys as a child?
2. What did you want to be when you grew up?
3. Is that what you are now?
4. Do you know any women with driving jobs?
5. Do you know any women who are doing "men's" jobs?
6. How do you feel about these changing times?

✍ Writing

1. Choose the correct words and fill in the blanks.

take	have	high
on	no	not
rates	auto	with

Every car owner must have _____ insurance. But everyone does

_____ pay the same rate. Good drivers with _____ traffic tickets or

accidents pay lower _____. Drivers _____ traffic tickets and accidents

_____ their record must pay _____ rates.

2. Fill in the grid below with your own information on the kinds of work you can do. Think about all your skills: things you learned at home or at school, and things you did as a volunteer or helper.

Job	Skills	Experience

Lesson 18 Activity Pages

A. Match the statement with the correct occupation.

1. I drive people around town in a 4–door sedan.   a. truck driver

2. I deliver pizzas.   b. delivery person

3. I drive people around town in a bus.   c. taxicab driver

4. I take produce to the big supermarkets.   d. bus driver

B. Look at the application form and answer the questions.

Personal Information

Pinos, Rafael   *7739 E. Linden Rd.,*   *Van Nuys, CA 91406*   *(818) 555-1325*

Driving experience:
    a. Own a car now?   Y   (N)
    b. Owned a car in your country?   Y   (N)
    c. Drive a truck?   (Y)   N
    d. Kind of truck   *pick-up*

Driver's license number: _____ *N0752640* _____

Driving record: (Good)   Poor   **Auto Insurance:** (Y)   N

1. Does Rafael have a driver's license?   _____

2. Is he a good driver?   _____

3. Does he have auto insurance?   _____

4. Did he drive in his country?   _____

5. What kind of truck does he drive now?   _____

6. What's his driver's license number?   _____

C. Fill out the application form with your information.

PANDORA'S PIZZA
Job Application

Personal Information

Last Name   First Name   Address   Phone

_____   _____   _____   _____

_____

Driving experience: _____

     a. Own a car now?   Y   N
     b. Owned a car in your country?   Y   N
     c. Drive a truck?   Y   N
     d. Kind of truck   _____

Driver's license number: _____

Driving record: Good   Poor   **Auto Insurance:**   Y   N

Skills:

     _____   cook _____ food

     _____   file

     _____   type

     _____   speak English

     _____   speak _____

     _____   wait tables

     _____   use a computer

Notes

I. Listening Comprehension

Listen and circle the correct answer, A or B.

1.

     A   B

2.

     A   B

3.

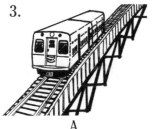 

     A   B

4.

     A   B

5.

     A   B

6.

     A   B

7.

A. Yes, he does.

B. Yes, he is.

8.

A. She drove a bus.

B. She drives a bus.

II. Reading

Circle the correct answer.

1. What kind of car _____ he need?

       do   does   can

2. I want a car _____ good condition.

       of   in   on

3. Did you _____ your car for work?

       buy   bought   buying

4. He _____ the car last month.

       buys   bought   buying

III. Writing

Fill in the blanks with the correct words.

bought	bus	buys	doesn't
drove	lives	walks	

Two years ago Linda lived in Milton, a small town. In Milton she _____ a compact

car and she _____ to work. Now Linda _____ in a big city, and she takes the

_____ to work. The bus stop is near her home. Sometimes she _____ to work.

She _____ need a car.

Unit Seven

Let's Go Shopping

SALE TODAY

MAIL ORDER FASHIONS

Would You Like to Try It On?

Objectives: In this lesson you will learn to go shopping for clothes.

✔ **Review:** Driver Occupations

1. Volunteers list as many driver occupations as you can.
2. Discuss: Do you need to have auto insurance?

   Are there any problems getting auto insurance?
3. Ask your neighbor: Do you have a good driving record?

Something New: Clothing Sizes

Women's Sizes (cardigans)

S (small)
32

M (medium)
34–36

L (large)
38–40

Men's Sizes (pullovers)

S (small)

M (medium)

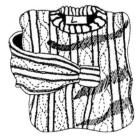
L (large)

XL (extra large)

☛ Practice: "It's a large (size)"

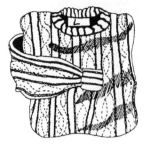

1. S1: What size is that blue sweater?
   S2: It's a men's large.

2. S1: Is that red cardigan a women's large?
   S2: No, it isn't. It's a small.

Let's Talk: Would You Like to Try It On?

Sue Duran is shopping for clothes today. She is at the sweater counter.

Sue: I'd like to see that yellow cardigan in a medium (size), please.

Salesperson: Here you are. Would you like to try it on?

Sue: Yes, I would. (Tries on the sweater.)

Salesperson: That looks good on you. How does it feel?

Sue: It fits perfectly. I'd like to buy it.

☛ Practice: "A small in black, please"

1. S1: What size sweater would you like to try on?
   S2: A small in black, please.

2. S1: I'd like to see a white pullover.
   S2: In what size?
   S1: An extra large.

3. S1: Does the small fit?

   S2: No, it doesn't. Please show me
a medium.

4. S1: How does the large fit?

   S2: It fits fine.

■ Interaction: Buying and Selling

Use real sweaters or pictures of sweaters. In groups, take turns as salesperson and customers for men's and women's sweaters.

Example: S1: I'm looking for a blue cardigan.

          S2: What size?

          S1: Men's small, please.

          S2: Here you are.

★ Something Extra: A T–Shirt Sale

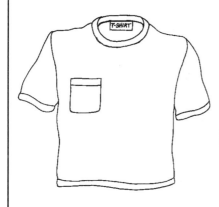

SALE! MEN'S AND WOMEN'S T-SHIRTS!

Were $15   100% Cotton   Now $10

SAVE!   Thursday Friday Saturday   **SAVE!**

SOLIDS AND STRIPES

Women's Colors

Solids

red   yellow   green   blue   purple

Stripes

red/white   blue/white

Men's Colors

Solids

blue   navy blue   beige   white

Stripes

navy/white   beige/white

☛ **Practice: "What's on sale?"**

1. S1: What's on sale this weekend?
   S2: Men's T–shirts.

2. S1: Are women's on sale, too?
   S2: Yes, they are.

3. S1: What color T–shirts do
       you plan to buy?
   S2: Blue and white.

4. S1: Do you plan to get solids
       or stripes?
   S2: I like stripes.

T–SHIRT SALE
Was $15
Now $10

5. S1: What was the original
       price of the shirts?
   S2: Fifteen dollars.

6. S1: What is the sale price?
   S2: It's ten dollars.

■ Interaction: How Much Did You Save?

Everyone wants to save money. Sometimes stores have special sales to get customers. Many people go to discount stores for special prices. Discuss these questions with your partner.

1. Are you wearing anything that you bought at a sale or at a discount store?
2. Are you waiting for a sale to buy something you want?
3. How do you learn about sales?
4. What ideas do you have for saving money?

Reading: Mail Order Shopping

Sue receives several mail order catalogs every week. These books advertise all kinds of items: clothing, housewares, gifts, jewelry, and toys, for example.

Everything looks so good. Sue would like to order many things. But Sue lives in a big city and can go shopping for all the items. The mail order catalogs are helpful to people with no place or time to shop.

Mail order shopping is convenient, but it costs more because of the postage.

Discussion

1. What is mail order shopping?
2. What can you buy through the mail?
3. Mail order shopping can be convenient for what kind of person?
4. What is the added cost of mail order shopping?
5. Do you receive many catalogs through the mail?
6. What do you do with them?

✍ Writing

THE SMART SHOP

Catalog #	Qty.	Description	Color	Size	Price	Total
1325	1	Men's cardigan	Navy	Sm.	30.00	30.00
2657	2	Men's T–shirts	Wht.	Lg.	13.00	26.00

Follow the examples and fill in the order form for the following:

   Cat. #786, 1 women's cardigan, medium, red, $25

   Cat. #578, 2 women's T–shirts, large, 1 blue, 1 red, $12

   Cat. #1567, 1 men's pullover, extra large, black, $25

   Cat. #2020, 1 men's wool scarf, beige, $20

Catalog #	Qty.	Description	Color	Size	Price	Total

Fill in the blanks:

1. I'm looking _____ a men's sweater.

   What _____ do you want?

   A large _____ navy.

2. Are men's white T–shirts _____ sale?

   Yes, _____ are.

   How _____ and _____ size would you like?

   I'd like two _____ size 40, please.

A. *Look at the sweaters, listen to the saleswoman, and write the correct prices on the tags.*

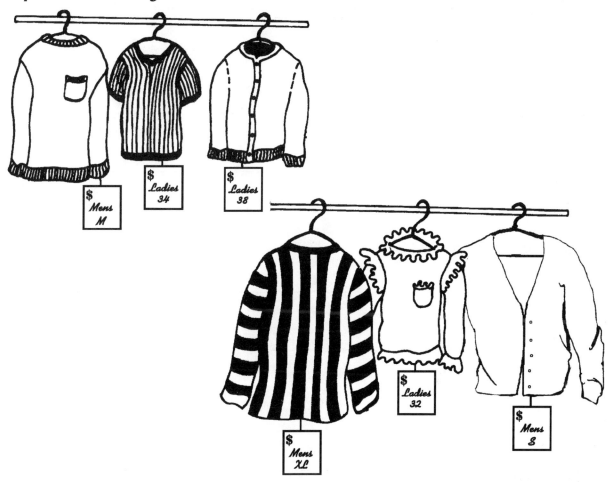

B. *Talk about the chart below with your partner.*

CUSTOMER	CLOTHING ITEM	SIZE	COLOR
Margaret	sweater	32	purple
Felix	T–shirt	XL	navy/white
Kathy	T–shirt	38	red
Sun Yong	sweater	M	beige

C. Look at the chart on page 185 and write the questions and answers.

1. What is Kathy looking for?

   She's looking for a red T-shirt.
   _____

2. What size does she need?

   _____

3. _____

   He's looking for a sweater.

4. What color does Sun Yong want?

   _____

5. _____

   She's looking for a sweater.

6. What color does she want?

   _____

7. What's Felix looking for?

   _____

8. What size does he need?

   _____

Notes

Do You Have a Receipt?

Objectives: In this lesson you will learn to exchange or to return items that you have bought.

✔ Review: Buying Clothing

Take turns acting as a salesperson and a customer looking for the following items:

women's cardigan, blue, medium

women's T–shirt, flowered, large

men's pullover, black/white, extra large

2 men's T–shirts, white, small

Examples: I'm looking for a women's cardigan.

Do you have men's T–shirts on sale today?

Something New: Too Small or Too Big
Listen and Look

too small

The T–shirt is too small.
too tight.
too short.

The pants are too small.
too tight.
too short.

too big

The T–shirt is too big.
      too loose.
      too long.
The pants are too big.
      too loose.
      too long.

Let's Talk: Do You Have a Receipt?

Maria bought a size 10 T–shirt for Peter yesterday. He tried it on, but it didn't fit. It was too small. Maria is at the department store to exchange the shirt.

Maria: I'd like to exchange this shirt, please. It's too small for my 8–year–old.

Salesperson: What size do you want?

Maria: I need a size 12. My son's big for his age.

Salesperson: Do you have your receipt?

Maria: Yes, I do. Here it is.

☛ **Practice: "It's too big for me"**

1. S1: I need to exchange this shirt.
   S2: What's wrong with it?
   S1: It's too big for me.

2. S1: Can I exchange these pants?
   S2: What's wrong with them?
   S1: They're too tight for me.

3. S1: I'd like to exchange this sweater.
   S2: Do you have the receipt?
   S1: Yes, I do.

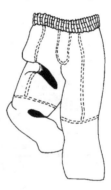

4. S1: These jeans are too small for my daughter.
   S2: Do you have the receipt?
   S1: Yes, I do.

5. S1: Did the sweater fit her?
   S2: No, it didn't. It was too tight.

6. S1: How do the jeans fit?
   S2: They fit just fine.

★ Something Extra: Store Policy

RECEIPT	
T–SHIRT	$9.95
TAX	.70
TOTAL	$10.65
NO CASH REFUNDS	

Customer: This T–shirt is too large.
I want my money back.

Salesclerk: I'm sorry, there are no refunds.
Look at your receipt.

THAT'S NOT FAIR

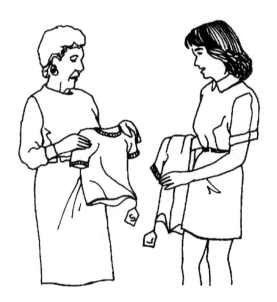

Salesclerk: But you can exchange that one for a small.
Customer: Okay. I'd like to do that.

☞ Practice: "I want to exchange this sweater"

1. S1: This shirt doesn't fit my grandmother.
   S2: Do you want a refund?
   S1: Yes. I'd like my money back.

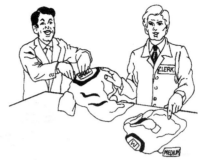

2. S1: I want to exchange this sweater.
   S2: What size do you need?
   S1: Medium.

3. S1: I'd like to return these pants.
   S2: I can give you credit, but I can't give you a refund.

4. S1: I'd like to exchange this blouse for that belt.
   S2: The belt is $5.00 less. You'll get a five-dollar credit.

Reading: Sue Was Lucky

Sue received a beautiful blue blouse as a birthday gift last week. She tried it on. It didn't fit. It was too big.

She didn't have the receipt. She went to the store and explained the problem. Sue was lucky. She was able to exchange the blouse for one in her size. It was the same style and same color.

Discussion

1. What was wrong with Sue's birthday gift?
2. What was her problem?
3. Why was Sue lucky?

✎ Writing

1. Choose the correct word and write it on the line.

   Even Exchange   Refund   Credit

   a. Return an item and receive cash.   _____

   b. Return a blue shirt for a red one

       with the same price.   _____

   c. Return an item and receive no cash.   _____

2. Complete the dialogue.

   Sachi needs to exchange her husband's sweater.

   Salesperson: May I help you?

   Sachi: I'd like _____ this sweater.

   Salesperson: What's wrong _____?

   Sachi: It's _____ big for _____.

Lesson 20 Activity Pages

A. *Listen to the customers complain about their new clothes. Circle the letter of the correct picture.*

1.   a   b   c

2.   a   b   c

3.   a   b   c

4.   a   b   c

5.   a   b   c

B. Listen to the customers try to return the items.

Listen to whether they want a credit, refund or even exchange and make a check under the correct column.

	Credit	Refund	Even Exchange
1. Joanne			
2. Craig			
3. Dick			
4. Betty			
5. Sam			

C. Talk with your partner.

Partner A look at this page. Partner B look at page 197.
Ask and answer the questions about the clothing.

Customer	Clothing Item	Reason for Return	Customer wants ...
Kitty	*dress*	small	a refund
Frank		too long	
Sara	sweater		an even exchange

D. Look at the pictures and put them in order.

Talk about the story you see.

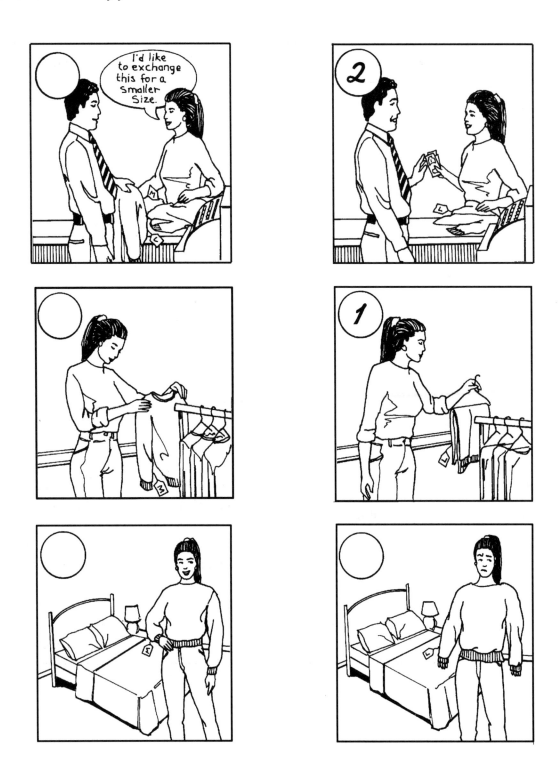

E. Look at the pictures on page 196 and write the missing words in the story.

big	bought	buys	exchanged	large
medium	returned	tried	was	

Last week Sara ___*went*___ to the store to buy a sweater. She always _____

a size large, so she _____ a _____ blue sweater. At home,

she _____ the sweater on. It was too _____! Sara's diet

was working! She _____ the sweater to the store and _____

it for a _____. Sara _____ very happy with her new sweater

and her new size.

F. Talk with your partner.

Partner B look at this page. Partner A look at C on page 195.
Ask and answer the questions about the clothing.

Customer	Clothing Item	Reason for Return	Customer wants...
Kitty	dress	small	*a refund*
Frank	pants		a credit
Sara		too tight	

They Feel a Little Tight

Objectives: In this lesson you will learn about buying and repairing shoes for the family.

✔ Review: Shopping Problems

Discuss and give suggestions for solving the following shopping problems:
You bought some clothes for your 10–year–old son last week, and …

1. The size 12 jeans are too tight. He needs a size 14.
2. He doesn't like the blue T–shirt. He wants a black one.
3. He doesn't want a sweater. He wants a jacket from another store.

Something New: Men's and Women's Shoes

	Dress Shoes	Work Shoes	Athletic Shoes
Women's			
Sizes	6A narrow	6B medium	6C wide
Men's			
Sizes	10A narrow	10B medium	10C wide

☛ Practice: "My shoes are 11B"

1. S1: What size are your shoes?
   S2: They're 7 narrow.

2. S1: What size shoes does she wear?
   S2: She wears a 6½B.

Let's Talk: They Feel a Little Tight

Tomas Gomez is looking for work shoes.

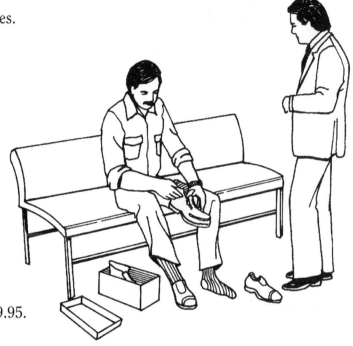

Tomas: I need some work shoes, size 11½B.

Salesperson: Try on this pair. How do they feel?

Tomas: They feel a little tight.

Salesperson: This pair is an 11½C. Try these on.

Tomas: They feel just right. How much are they?

Salesperson: They're on sale for $49.95.

Tomas: Great! I'll take them.

☛ Practice: "I need some work shoes"

1. S1: What kind of shoes do you need?
   S2: I need a pair of running shoes.

2. S1: What kind of shoes is she looking for?
   S2: She's looking for some dress shoes.

3. S1: What size shoes do you wear?
   S2: I wear a 7½B.

4. S1: How do these feel?
   S2: They feel very comfortable.

5. S1: What size did you try on?
   S2: I tried on a 7A.
   S1: Did they fit?
   S2: They fit just fine.

6. S1: Did the loafers fit him?
   S2: Yes they did.
   S1: What size were they?
   S2: They were a 10C.

★ Something Extra: Shoe Repair

Customer: My shoes are too tight.
Shoeman: I can stretch them for you.

Customer: Can you fix these heels?
Shoeman: I can put on taps.

Customer: Can you replace the heels?
            These are worn out.
Shoeman: Yes, Ma'am. They'll look like new.

Customer: My shoes are too loose.
They keep falling off.
Shoeman: Maybe you need insoles.

Customer: I don't want brown boots anymore.
I want black boots.
Shoeman: We can dye them for you.

Shoeman: Tell your dad he needs new soles.
Boy: How much is that?

Customer: Do you sell shoe laces?
Shoeman: We sure do. How long?

Customer: How much is it to dye my wedding shoes pink?
Shoeman: About $20.

☛ Practice Activity: What's the matter with these shoes?

Look at the pictures and write answers to the shoeman's questions. Then share your answers with a partner.

1. What size is the shoe?

   It's a 7½ B.

2. What's the matter with this shoe?

   _____

3. Why do you want me to add an insole?

   _____

4. Why do you want me to dye your shoes?

   _____

5. What's the matter with these shoes?

   _____

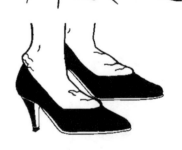

6. Are your shoes comfortable now?

   _____

■ Interaction: Shoe Repair

Ask the students in your group about their shoes.

> **Examples:** Are your shoes comfortable?
>
> Are your shoes in good condition?

Discuss shoe problems.

Make suggestions for solutions.

Reading: Shoes for the Family

The Casado family is at the shoe store today. Everyone in the family needs a pair of shoes.

The children wear their sneakers every day and don't like dress shoes. But the family is going to a wedding next week, so they have to buy some new shoes for Lucy and Ricky.

Mr. Casado needs work shoes. Mrs. Casado wants a pair of red shoes to match her new red dress. She wants to wear them to the wedding.

Discussion

1. Who needs to buy shoes today?
2. Why do the children need dress shoes?
3. Why do they like to wear sneakers?
4. What kind of shoes are most comfortable for you?

✍ Writing

Fill in the blanks:

All the Casados need _____ shoes today. Mr. Casado needs

_____ shoes. Mrs. Casado wants _____ shoes to match her

dress. The children need _____ shoes, but they are not happy. They

like to _____ sneakers.

A. Match the sentences with the problems.

1. I wear a size 6B, these are 6A.   _____ a. They're too big.

2. I wear a size 7, these are size 9.   _____ b. They're too wide.

3. I wear a size 8, but these are size 7.   _____ c. They're too small.

4. I wear a size 11B, but these are an 11C.   _____ d. They're too narrow.

B. Read the statements and make the questions.

Ask and answer the questions with your classmates.

1. Find someone who sears a size 7½ shoe.

   Do you wear a size 7½?   Name _____

2. Find someone who wears a size 10 shoe.

   _____   Name _____

3. Find someone who has a narrow foot.

   _____   Name _____

4. Find someone who has a wide foot.

   _____   Name _____

Unit Seven Evaluation

I. Listening Comprehension

Listen and circle the correct answer, A or B.

1.
A   B

2.
A   B

3.
A   B

4.
A   B

5.
A   B

6.
A   B

7.
A. Yes, it does.
B. No it doesn't.

8.
A. Yes, it is.
B. No, it isn't.

II. Reading

Circle the correct answer.

1. This sweater is too small.

   I want to _____ it.

        put on   exchange   buy

2. These pants don't fit.

   They're too _____.

        new   old   long

3. Try _____ this pair
   of shoes.

        at   on   in

4. Are your shoes comfortable?

   Yes, they _____.

        do   are   feel

III. Writing

Write the questions or answers.

Jan is looking for a pair of work pants. There's a big sale at the Blake Company now. Pants are on sale for $29.95. T–shirts are only $15.00.

1. What does Jan need to buy?

   _____

2. What kind of pants is she looking for?

   _____

3. _____

   They're $29.95.

4. _____

   They're $15.00.

5. _____

   It's at the Blake Company.

Unit Eight

Looking Good

Lesson 22

I'm Going to Get a Haircut

Objectives: In this lesson you will learn about getting service at a beauty or barber shop.

✔ Review: Buying Shoes

1. In pairs, take roles of customer and salesperson to buy:
    running shoes for yourself
    work shoes for a man/woman
2. Take roles of customer and shoe repairman to discuss the following problems:
    broken shoe laces, tight shoes
    worn–out soles, loose shoes

Something New: Beauty Shop Services

haircut

shampoo

blow dry

set

permanent (perm)

dye   manicure   pedicure

Discussion

1. Do you fix your own hair?
2. Do you ever go to a beauty shop?
3. What do you go to a beauty shop for?

Let's Talk: I'm Going to Get a Haircut

It's Saturday. May Lei and her husband Tom are making plans.

Tom: What are you going to do today?

May Lei: I'm going to get a haircut.

Tom: I need a haircut, too. Shall I go with you?

May Lei: I don't think so. I'm going to have a manicure and a pedicure, too.

Tom: I'm glad I asked. I'm not going to wait in a beauty shop all day. I have work to do.

☞ Practice: "I'm going to need a perm next month"

1. S1: Come on. I'm going to wash your hair.

   S2: I like how you wash my hair.

2. S1: I'm going to be 50 in September.

   S2: Darling, you look fabulous!

3. S1: I'm going to write a check, okay?

    S2: We don't usually accept checks. But, it's okay this time.

4. S1: I'm going to need a perm next month.

    S2: Do you want to make an appointment?

Something New: Barber Shop Services

moustache

gel

beard

goatee

clipper

sideburns

Discussion

Do you know anyone who has a moustache?

　　　　　　　　　　a beard?

　　　　　　　　　　sideburns?

　　　　　　　　　　a goatee?

　　　　　　　　　　a radical haircut?

Let's Talk: My Wife's Going to Be There All Day

May Lei's husband, Tom, decided to go to the barber shop by himself.

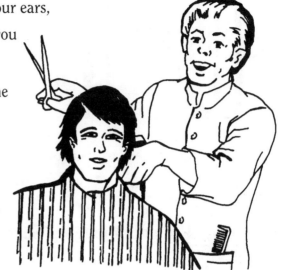

Barber: I'm going to cut the hair in your ears, trim your eyebrows and give you a haircut in 15 minutes.

Tom: That's great! I want to go home and watch the game.

Barber: Where's your wife?

Tom: She's getting a haircut. But she's going to be there all day.

Barber: Sometimes it's better to be a man!

☛ Practice: "What are you going to do?"

1. S1: I'm going to put some gel in your hair.
   S2: Awesome.

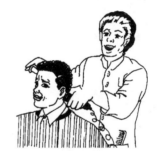

2. S1: I'm going to buzz this hair.
   S2: I'm going to be cool.

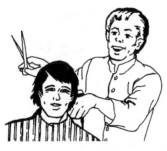

3. S1: When are you going to finish?
   S2: I'm going to finish in 15 minutes.

4. S1: What are you going to do when you go home?
   S2: I'm going to watch the game.

★ Something Extra: Where Are You Going Tomorrow?

Hairdresser: Where are you going tomorrow?
Customer: I'm going to a barbecue.

☞ Practice: "I'm going jogging Saturday"

1. S1: Where are you going Saturday?
   S2: I'm going jogging.

2. S1: Where are you going to school next year?
   S2: I'm going to UCLA.

3. S1: Where are you going?
   S2: I'm going to pick up the kids.

4. S1: Am I going for the pizza?
   S2: Do you have gas in your car?

Reading: Times Change

Once, men only went to barber shops. Women only went to beauty shops.

A red, white and blue barber pole identified a barber shop. Haircuts were cheap. The shop was like a club for men who talked about sports and smoked cigars.

Then, women discovered short hair, cheap haircuts, and fast service. Barbers had new customers! Men discovered beauty shop services. They got permanents, dyed their hair and got manicures.

What's going to happen next?

✍ Writing

going	blows	beauty	cuts
go	permanents	be	

When I go to the _____ shop, I get a shampoo first. Then, the stylist

_____ my hair and _____ it dry. I always feel terrific when

I go home.

I think I'm going to _____ back to school. I'm _____ to

study how to be a hair stylist. I like making people look great. I don't think I

want to give _____ though. They smell bad.

I wonder who my first customer is going to _____. Any volunteers?

A. *Listen to the customers tell the receptionist what they'd like.*

Circle the letter of the correct picture.

1.

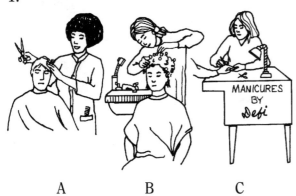

A   B   C

2.

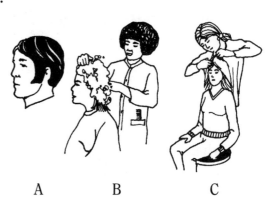

A   B   C

3.

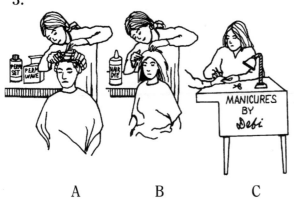

A   B   C

4.

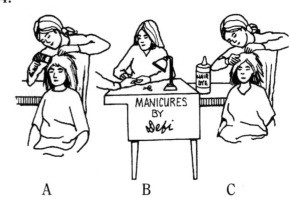

A   B   C

5.

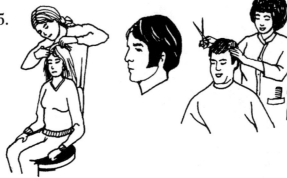

A   B   C

B. Look at yesterday's schedule for Alberta's Beauty Salon.

Ask and answer the questions below with your partner.

Who came in at...?   Who got a...?   Who saw...?

Operator	9:00 a.m.	10:00 a.m.	11:00 a.m.
Barbara	Miller/haircut	Allen/shampoo & set	
Jose	Smith/perm		Carlson/dye
Carmen	Foster/manicure	Watson/pedicure	

C. Look at the schedule above and write the questions and answers.

1. Who is going to shampoo Ms. Allen's hair?

   _____

2. What is Ms. Miller going to get?

   _____

3. Who is going to come in at 11?

   _____

4. What time is Ms. Foster going to come in?

   _____

5. _____

   She is going to get a manicure at 10.

6. _____

   Jose is going to dye her hair.

7. _____

   She is going to come in at 9 for a perm.

8. _____

   Mrs. Carlson is going to come in at 11.

Unit Eight | **Lesson 23**

Special Occasions

Objectives: In this lesson you will learn to talk about special occasions.

✔ Review: Beauty and Barber Shops

1. As a class, demonstrate the services that a beauty shop and a barber shop offer: Shampoo, set, blow dry, haircut, dye, permanent, manicure, pedicure, shave, trim and hair styling.

2. In pairs, act out a customer discussing services with an operator.

    Example: Can I get a manicure?

Something New: Celebrations

birthday

wedding

wedding anniversary

retirement

bridal shower

baby shower

Let's Talk: Surprise!

Class is almost over. Sue and Tony slip out of the room, then return with a birthday cake and candles.

Class: Surprise!

Happy birthday, Mei!

Mei: Oh my goodness!

What a beautiful cake!

Sue: (handing a gift to Mei)

And here's a little present from your friends.

Mei: For me? I don't know what to say.

Tony: Just make a wish and blow out the candles. Then we can all

have a piece of cake.

☛ Practice Activity: What can you say?

What can you say when you are surprised?

You are happy and embarrassed at the same time.

Some possible responses:

What a nice/big/great/wonderful surprise!

Thank you so much!

I'm speechless!

★ Something Extra: Compliments

What can you say when you receive a compliment? The best response: "Thank you."

Other possible responses:

S1: That's a beautiful scarf.

S2: Thank you. It was a birthday gift.

S1: Your baby is beautiful.

S2: Thank you. She's a good baby.

S1: Your car looks great.

S2: Thanks. I just washed and waxed it.

S1: You speak English very well.

S2: Thank you. I try.

☛ Practice Activity: Giving and Receiving Compliments

With a partner, practice giving and receiving compliments for the following situations:

1. a new hairdo
2. good work at the workplace
3. a good speech in class
4. new clothing

Let's Talk: Let's Have a Baby Shower for Layne

Rosa: I want to have a baby shower for Layne.

Maria: Great! Let me help!

Rosa: No. She doesn't want a party.

Maria: Why?

Rosa: She doesn't want any gifts.

Maria: I'm not going to listen to her. What are you going to get her?

☛ Practice: "What are you going to give her?"

1. S1: What are you going to give her?
   S2: I'm going to make a blanket.

2. S1: What is she going to have?
   S2: She's going to have a boy.

3. S1: What is your brother going to do?
   S2: He's going to write a song for the baby.

4. S1: What are the Harpers going to do?
   S2: They're going to paint the baby's room.

Reading: A Bridal Shower

Emily's wedding is in June. Last Sunday, Emily's friends gave her a bridal shower. Twenty of her close friends and relatives were at the party.

It was a kitchen shower, so all the presents were for Emily's new kitchen. She received dishes, pot and pans, an iron and an ironing board, a broom and a mop, lots of bowls, and several cookbooks.

Everyone played games, then had refreshments of sandwiches, salads, and desserts. It was a happy party for bride–to–be Emily.

Discussion

1. What is a bridal shower?
2. What kind of presents did Emily receive?
3. What happened at the shower?
4. Are showers just for women?

✍ Writing

Write the questions or answers or responses.

1. Who came to Emily's shower?

   _____

2. What kind of shower was it?

   _____

3. _____

   He's going to write a song for the baby.

4. _____

   She's going to have a boy.

5. Your scarf is very pretty.

   _____

A. Something special just happened to each of these women.

Listen and see if you can tell who is talking.
Put the correct numbers under the people.

B. Draw a line from the compliment to the answer.

1. That's a beautiful baby.

2. That's a beautiful scarf.

3. Your hair looks great.

4. Your English is very good!

5. This soup is delicious.

6. You did a great job!

a. Thanks, I just got it.

b. Thank you. It's a beautiful language.

c. I'm glad you like it.

d. Thank you. I got a haircut.

e. Thanks, we all worked together.

f. Thank you. He's our pride and joy.

C. Label the "photos" below with the titles in the box. Have fun!

Good Job!   Great Hair!   Beautiful Baby!   Nice Hat!   Terrific Weather!

_____   _____

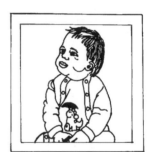

_____   _____

_____

D. Talk about the picture.

E. Look at the picture above and complete the story.

50	anniversary	bought	had
gave	gifts	good	got
prepared	together	was	wasn't

Today was Max and Edie's 50th _anniversary_ . They were married _____

years ago. Their friends _____ them a surprise anniversary party. They

_____ a beautiful cake, _____ some snacks, and made a fruit punch.

Max _____ very surprised, but Edie _____. They liked their

_____, especially their T–shirts. Max and Edie _____ a good time at

the party. They danced and laughed a lot. It was a very _____ way to

celebrate their years _____.

F. Change the statements into questions.

Ask and answer the questions with your classmates.
Write the names of your classmates who answer "yes" on the correct lines.

1. Find someone who had a birthday last month.

    Did you have a birthday last month?   Name _____

2. Find someone who went to a baby shower last year.

    _____   Name _____

3. Find someone who had a wedding anniversary last year.

    _____   Name _____

4. Find someone who came to the United States last year.

    _____   Name _____

Lesson 24

Greeting Cards

Objectives: In this lesson you will learn to choose appropriate greeting cards for special occasions.

✔ Review: Special Occasions

1. With your classmates, identify and discuss some special occasions: Birthday, wedding, wedding anniversary, and retirement.

   How do we generally celebrate birthdays? wedding anniversaries? retirements? Describe weddings in your native country.

2. In groups, practice giving and receiving compliments.
   Example: S1: That's a good–looking jacket.
   S2: Thanks. It's warm.
   Etc.

Something New: Cards for Special Occasions

Happy Birthday!

Best Wishes!

Congratulations!

Thank You

Get Well Soon!

In Sympathy

Happy Mother's Day!

Be My Valentine

Let's Talk: We're Going to Get Him a Card

Sara Gomez is telling the class about their classmate, Ben Lee.

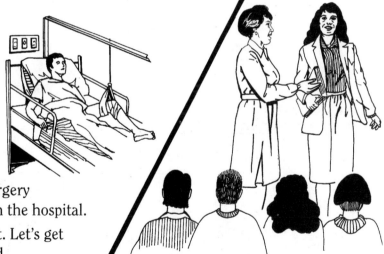

Sara: Ben Lee had knee surgery yesterday. He's still in the hospital.

Mrs. Baker: I'm sorry to hear that. Let's get him a "Get Well" card.

Sara: I'll buy it! Then, we can each write a special message inside.

Victor: When is he going to get out of the hospital?

Sara: In about a week, I think.

☛ Practice: "He needs back surgery"

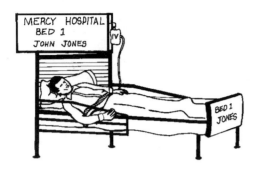 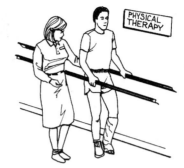

1. S1: Where's John going?
   S2: He's going to the hospital.
   S1: What's the matter?
   S2: He needs back surgery.

2. S1: Is Aram going to the hospital?
   S2: Yes, he is.
   S1: What are they going to do to him?
   S2: They're going to give him physical therapy.

3. S1: When is Dora going to leave the hospital?
   S2: In a few days.

4. S1: When are you going to go to work?
   S2: In a few minutes.

★ Something Extra: Messages

Happy Birthday!

Greeting cards have special messages inside.

■ Interaction: Messages

1. Can you think of other messages for the special occasions listed on page 229?

2. Talk with your group and write as many messages as you can.

3. When the teacher calls time, each group will read its messages. The teacher will record them on the board.

Reading: Having a Wonderful Time

 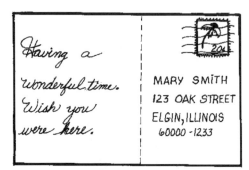

Every summer we receive picture postcards from around the world. Our vacationing friends send us cards from all over the United States, like San Francisco, New York City, Miami Beach, and Hawaii. Some cards come from Acapulco, Rome, and Hong Kong.

These cards show pictures of beautiful beaches, waterfalls, big cities, and hotels. They all say, "Having a wonderful time. Wish you were here."

The postal system around the world is very slow. Our traveling friends are back home long before their cards arrive.

Discussion

1. Who sends picture postcards?

2. What kind of pictures are on the postcards?

3. Did you receive any postcards this year?

4. Where were they from?

5. Did you send any cards this year? If so, from where?

6. Who got home first—you or the postcards?

✎ Writing

Write inside–the–card messages for the following situations.

1. Carla is 7 today.

   Have a fun day today!
   _____

2. Yoko and Ken had a baby last week.

   _____

3. Ben's father died a couple of days ago.

   _____

4. You had a wonderful dinner at the Wongs.

   _____

5. Russo and Maria are getting married.

   _____

6. Ben Lee had knee surgery.

   _____

A. Read the situations and write the number next to the correct card.

1. It's my aunt's birthday. _____ a.

2. My father–in–law is very ill. _____ b.

3. My friend just had a new baby! _____ c.

4. February 14th is coming. _____ d.

5. I just got a beautiful birthday gift. _____ e.

6. My friends just got married. _____ f.

B. Look at the pictures. Tell the story with your partner.

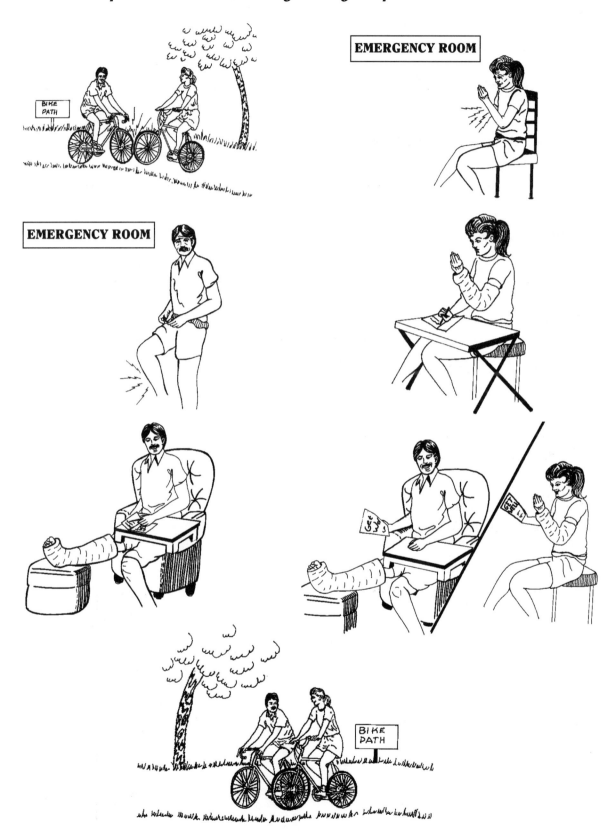

EMERGENCY ROOM

EMERGENCY ROOM

BIKE PATH

BIKE PATH

C. Look at the pictures and write the questions and answers.

1. What happened to the man and woman?

   They had an accident.

2. What's the matter with the man?

   _____

3. What's the matter with the woman?

   _____

4. _____

   He got a get–well card.

5. _____

   Yes, she did.

6. Did they see each other again?

   _____

Unit Eight Evaluation

I. Listening Comprehension

Listen and circle the correct answer, A or B.

1.

    A   B

2.

    A   B

3.

    A   B

4.

    A   B

5.

    A   B

6.

    A   B

7.

A. Yes, she had.

B. Yes, she did.

8.

A. Thank you.

B. No. It's just a sale scarf.

II. Reading

Circle the correct answer.

1. _____ me a haircut, please.

    Trim   Give   Cut

2. I'm _____ to go tomorrow.

    not   going   be

3. Here's a little present from _____ friends.

    you   your   yours

4. Ben's in the hospital. I'm sorry to _____ that.

    hear   heard   hearing

III. Writing

Fill in the blanks with the correct words.

after	before	here	in	is
on	received	letter	postcard	returned
there	time	travel	was	going

Yesterday, I _____ a postcard from Paris. It _____ from

Yvonne. She went to Europe last month _____ her honeymoon.

The _____ said: "Having a wonderful _____. Wish you were

_____."

Yvonne _____ from Europe last week. She reached home _____

her postcard did! I'm not _____ to tell her.